The Aquarian Sun Sign Guides

LEO

Bernard Fitzwalter has been interested in astrology since he was about six, when he played King Herod's astrologer in his primary school nativity play. For the past six years he has been teaching astrology for the Marylebone-Paddington Institute, and for seven years he has had a regular column in OVER 21 magazine. In 1984 he appeared in the first series of Anglia Television's *Zodiac Game*, which prompted the *Daily Mirror* to say that he was 'enough to give astrology a good name'.

AQUARIAN SUN SIGN GUIDES

LEO

23 JULY ~ 22 AUGUST

Bernard Fitzwalter

Cover illustration by Steinar Lund
Cover typography by Steven Lee

THE AQUARIAN PRESS
Wellingborough, Northamptonshire

First published 1987

British Library Cataloguing in Publication Data

Fitzwalter, Bernard
Leo.—(The Aquarian sun sign guides)
1. Zodiac
I. Title
133.5'4   BF1728.A2

ISBN 0-85030-576-4

*The Aquarian Press is part of the
Thorsons Publishing Group*

Printed and bound in Great Britain

Contents

PART 4: LEO TRIVIA

Introduction

This book has been written to help you find out a little about astrology and a lot about yourself. It explains, for the first time, the motives and aims that guide your actions and make you do things the way you do; what it does not do is give you a list of 'typical Leo' things to see if you recognize any of them. You are not likely to be typical anything: you are unique. What you *do* have in common with others who have birthdays at about the same time as you is a way of using your energy, a way of thinking, a set of motives and beliefs which seem to make sense to you, and which other people, those of the other eleven signs, obviously do not have. This book shows you those motives and beliefs, and shows you how they fit in with those of the other eleven signs. The zodiac is like a jigsaw: all the pieces have to be there for the whole picture to emerge.

This book also sets out to answer some very simple questions which are often asked but seldom answered. Questions like 'Why does the zodiac have twelve signs?' and 'What does being a Leo actually mean?' as well as 'Why are Leos supposed to be generous? Why can't they be mean instead? and why don't all the people of the same star sign look the same?'

The reason that these questions are seldom answered is because all too many astrologers don't know the rudiments of astrological theory, and what they do know they don't tell, because they think it is too difficult for the man in the street to understand. This is obvious nonsense: astrology was devised for and by people who did not normally read or write as much as we do, nor did they all have PhDs or the equivalent. The man in the street is quite capable of understanding anything provided that it is shown simply and clearly, from first principles upwards, and provided he has sufficient interest. Buying this book is evidence enough of your interest, and I hope that the explanations are simple enough and clear enough for you. If they are not, it is my fault, and not that of astrology.

How to Use this Book

The book is in four parts. It is best to read them in sequence, but if you have neither time nor patience, then they each work individually. Part 2 does not assume that you have read Part 1, though it helps. Part 3 makes a lot more sense if you have already read Parts 1 and 2, but it isn't mandatory. Part 4, although just as firmly based on astrological principles as the other three, is deliberately intended as light relief.

The first part of the book deals with the theory behind the zodiac; it sets out the principles of astrology and enables you to see why Leo is assigned the qualities it has, how the ruling planet system works, and what all the other signs are like in terms of motivation, so you can compare them to your own. There is a short and effective method given for assessing the aims and motives of other people. When you read Part 3 you will need to know a bit about the other signs, as you will be finding out that you have more to you than just the Leo part you knew about.

The second part describes the essential Leo. It shows you how there are different sorts of Leos according to where your birthday falls in the month, and shows how Leonine energy is used differently in the Leo as a child, adult, and a parent.

Since you spend the greatest part of your life in dealing with other individuals, the way Leo deals with relationships is treated in some detail. This is the largest section of the book.

The third part shows you a different kind of zodiac, and enables you to go into your own life in much greater detail. It isn't complicated, but you do need to think. It crosses the border between the kind of astrology you get in the magazines, and the sort of thing a real astrologer does. There's no reason why you can't do it yourself because, after all, you know yourself best.

The fourth part shows you the surface of being a Leo, and how that zodiacal energy comes out in your clothes, your home, even your favourite food. The final item of this part actually explains the mechanics of being lucky, which you probably thought was impossible.

I hope that when you finish reading you will have a clearer view of yourself, and maybe like yourself a little more. Don't put the book away and forget about it; read it again in a few months' time—you will be surprised at what new thoughts about yourself it prompts you to form!

Note

Throughout this book, the pronouns 'he', 'him', and 'his' have been used to describe both male and female. Everything which applies to a male Leo applies to a female Leo as well. There are two reasons why I have not bothered to make the distinction: firstly, to avoid long-windedness; secondly, because astrologically there is no need. It is not possible to tell from a horoscope whether the person to whom it relates is male or female, because to astrology they are both living individuals full of potential.

BERNARD FITZWALTER

Part 1

How the Zodiac Works

1. The Meaning of the Zodiac

Two Times Two is Four; Four Times Three is Twelve

It is no accident that there are twelve signs in the zodiac, although there are a great many people who reckon themselves to be well versed in astrology who do not know the reasons why, and cannot remember ever having given thought to the principles behind the circle of twelve.

The theory is quite simple, and once you are familiar with it, it will enable you to see the motivation behind all the other signs as well as your own. What's more, you only have to learn nine words to do it. That's quite some trick—being able to understand what anybody else you will ever meet is trying to do, with nine words.

It works like this.

The zodiac is divided into twelve signs, as you know. Each of the twelve represents a stage in the life cycle of solar energy as it is embodied in the life of mankind here on our planet. There are tides in this energy; sometimes it flows one way, sometimes another, like the tides of the ocean. Sometimes it is held static, in the form of an object, and sometimes it is released when that object is broken down after a period of time. The twelve signs show all these processes, both physical and spiritual, in their interwoven pattern.

Six signs are used to show the flowing tide, so to speak, and six for the ebbing tide. Aries, Gemini, Leo, Libra, Sagittarius, and Aquarius are the 'flowing' group, and the others form the second group. You will notice at once that the signs alternate, one with the other, around the zodiac, so that the movement is maintained, and there is never a concentration of one sort of energy in one place. People whose Sun sign is in the first group tend to radiate their energies outwards from themselves. They are the ones who like to make the first move, like to be the ones to take command of a situation, like to put something of themselves into whatever they are doing. They don't feel right standing on the sidelines; they are the original have-a-go types. Energy comes out of them and is radiated towards other people, in the same way as the Sun's energy is radiated out to the rest of the solar system.

The people in the other signs are the opposite to that, as you would expect. They collect all the energy from the first group, keeping it for themselves and making sure none is wasted. They absorb things from a situation or from a personal contact, rather than contributing to it. They prefer to watch and learn rather than make the first move. They correspond to the Moon, which collects and reflects the energy of the Sun. One group puts energy out, one group takes it back in. The sum total of energy in the universe remains constant, and the two halves of the zodiac gently move to and fro with the tide of the energies.

This energy applies both to the real and concrete world of objects, as well as to the intangible world of thoughts inside our heads.

A distinction has to be made, then, between the real world and the intangible world. If this is done, we have four kinds of energy: outgoing and collecting, physical and mental. These four kinds of energy have been recognized for a long time, and were given names to describe the way they work more than two thousand years ago. These are the elements. All the energy in the cosmos can be described in the terms of these four: Fire, Earth, Air, Water.

Fire is used to describe that outgoing energy which applies to the real and physical world. There are three signs given to it: Aries, Leo, and Sagittarius. People with the Sun in any of these signs find themselves with the energy to get things going. They are at their best when making a personal contribution to a situation, and they expect to see some tangible results for their efforts. They are sensitive to the emotional content of anything, but that is not their prime concern, and so they tend to let it look after itself while they busy themselves with the actual matter in hand. Wherever you meet Fire energy in action, it will be shown as an individual whose personal warmth and enthusiasm are having a direct effect on his surroundings.

Earth is used to describe the real and physical world where the energies are being collected and stored, sometimes in the form of material or wealth. The three signs given to the element are Taurus, Virgo, and Capricorn. Where Fire energy in people makes them want to move things, Earth energy makes them want to hold things and stop them moving. The idea of touching and holding, and so that of possession, is important to these people, and you can usually see it at work in the way they behave towards their own possessions. The idea is to keep things stable, and to hold energy stored for some future time when it will be released. Earth Sun people work to ensure that wherever they are is secure and unlikely to change; if possible they would like the strength and wealth of their situation to increase, and will work towards that goal. Wherever you meet Earth energy in action, there will be more work being done than idle chat, and there will be a resistance to any kind of new idea. There will be money being made, and accumulated. The idea of putting down roots and bearing fruit may be a useful one to keep in mind when trying to understand the way this energy functions.

Air is used to describe outgoing mental energies; put more simply, this is communication. Here the ideas are formed in the mind of the individual, and put out in the hope that they can influence and meet the ideas of another individual; this is communication, in an abstract sense. Gemini, Libra, and Aquarius are all Air signs, and people with the Sun in those signs are very much concerned with communicating their energies to others. Whether anything gets done as a result of all the conversation is not actually important; if there is to be a concrete result, then that is the province of Fire or Earth energies. Here the emphasis is on shaping the concept, not the reality. There is an affinity with Fire energies, because both of them are outgoing, but other than that they do not cross over into each other's territory. Wherever you meet Air energy in action, there is a lot of talk, and new ideas are thrown up constantly, but there is no real or tangible result, no real product, and no emotional involvement; were there to be emotional content, the energies would be watery ones.

Water is the collection of mental energies. It is the response to communication or action. It absorbs and dissolves everything else, and puts nothing out. In a word, it is simply feelings. Everything emotional is watery by element, because it is a response to an outside stimulus, and is often not communicated. It is not, at least not in its pure sense, active or initiatory, and it does not bring anything into being unless transformed into energy of a different type, such as Fire. Cancer, Scorpio and Pisces are the Water signs, and natives of those signs are often moody, withdrawn, and uncommunicative. Their energy collects the energy of others, and keeps their mental responses to external events stored. They are not being sad for any particular reason; it is simply the way that energy works. It is quite obvious that they are not showing an outgoing energy, but neither have they anything tangible to show for their efforts, like the money and property which seem to accumulate around Earth people. Water people simply absorb, keep to themselves, and do not communicate. To the onlooker, this appears unexciting, but there again the onlooker is biased: Fire and Air energies only appreciate outgoing energy forms, Earth energies recognize material rather than mental energies, and other Water energies are staying private and self-contained!

We now recognize four kinds of energy. Each of these comes in three distinct phases; if one zodiac sign is chosen to represent each of these phases within an element, there would be twelve different kinds of energy, and that would define the zodiac of twelve, with each one showing a distinct and different phase of the same endless flow of energy.

The first phase, not surprisingly, is a phase of definition, where the energies take that form for the first time, and where they are at their purest; they are not modified by time or circumstance, and what they aim to do is to start things in their own terms. These four most powerful signs (one for each element, remember) are called cardinal signs: Aries, Cancer, Libra, Capricorn. When the Sun enters any of these signs, the seasons change; the first day of the Sun's journey through Aries is the first day of spring, and the Spring equinox; Libra marks the Autumnal equinox, while Cancer and Capricorn mark Mid-summer's Day and the shortest day respectively.

The second phase is where the energy is mature, and spreads itself a little; it is secure in its place, and the situation is well established, so there is a sort of thickening and settling of the energy flow. Here it is at its most immobile, even Air. The idea is one of maintenance and sustenance, keeping things going and keeping them strong. This stage is represented by Taurus, Leo, Scorpio, and Aquarius, and they are called, unsurprisingly, fixed signs. These four signs, and their symbols, are often taken to represent the four winds and the four directions North, South, East and West. Their symbols (with an eagle instead of a scorpion for Scorpio) turn up all over Europe as tokens for the evangelists Luke, Mark, John and Matthew (in that order).

The final phase is one of dissolution and change, as the energy finds itself applied to various purposes, and in doing so is changed into other forms. There is an emphasis on being used for the good, but being used up nonetheless. The final four signs are Gemini, Virgo, Sagittarius, and Pisces; in each of them the energies of their element are given back out for general use and benefit from where they had been maintained in the fixed phase. It is this idea of being used and changed which leads to this phase being called mutable.

Three phases of energy, then; one to form, one to grow strong and mature, and one to be used, and to become, at the end, something else. Like the waxing, full, and waning phases of the Moon.

The diagram on page 16 shows the twelve signs arranged in

their sequence round the zodiac. Notice how cleverly the cycle and phases interweave:

(a) Outgoing and collecting energies alternate, with no two the same next to each other;

(b) Physical ebb and flow are followed by mental ebb and flow alternately in pairs round the circle, meaning that the elements follow in sequence round the circle three times;

(c) Cardinal, fixed, and mutable qualities follow in sequence round the circle four times, and yet

(d) No two elements or qualities the same are next to each other, even though their sequences are not broken.

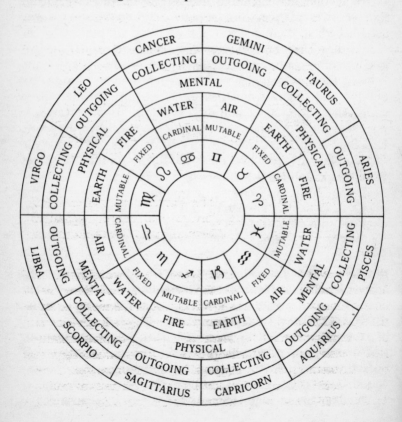

The interweaving is perfect. The zodiac shows all forms of energy, physical and mental, outgoing or incoming, waxing or waning, harmoniously forming a perfectly balanced unity when all the components are taken together. Humanity, as a whole, contains all the possibilities; each individual is a component necessary to the whole.

All this can be a bit long-winded when what you want is some way of holding all that information for instant recall and use, which is where the nine words come in.

If a single word is used for the kind of energy flow, and another two for the element and quality, then they can be used to form a sentence which will describe the way the energy is being used.

As a suggestion (use other words if they are more meaningful to you), try 'outgoing' and 'collecting' for the energy flows.

Next, for the elements:

Fire	:	activity	(Aries, Leo, Sagittarius)
Earth	:	material	(Taurus, Virgo, Capricorn)
Air	:	communication	(Gemini, Libra, Aquarius)
Water	:	feelings	(Cancer, Scorpio, Pisces)

And for the qualities:

Cardinal	:	defining	(Aries, Cancer, Libra, Capricorn)
Fixed	:	maintaining	(Taurus, Leo, Scorpio, Aquarius)
Mutable	:	using	(Gemini, Virgo, Sagittarius, Pisces)

Now in answer to the question 'What is a Gemini doing?' and answer can be formed as 'He's outgoing, and he's using communication', which neatly encapsulates the motivation of the sign. All that you need to know about the guiding principles of a Gemini individual, no matter who he is, is in that sentence. He will never deviate from that purpose, and you can adapt your own actions to partner or oppose his intention as you please.

A Scorpio? He's collecting, and he's maintaining his feelings. An Arian? He's outgoing, and he's defining activity. And so on.

Those nine words, or some similar ones which you like better, can be used to form effective and useful phrases which describe the motivation of everybody you will ever meet. How different people show it is their business, but their motivation and purpose is clear if you know their birthday.

Remember, too, that this motivation works at all levels, from the immediate to the eternal. The way a Taurean conducts himself in today's problems is a miniature of the way he is trying to achieve his medium-term ambitions over the next two or three years. It is also a miniature of his whole existence: when, as an old man, he looks back to see what he tried to do and what he achieved, both the efforts and the achievement, whatever it is, can be described in the same phrase with the same three words.

2. The Planets and the Horseshoe

You will have heard, or read, about the planets in an astrological context. You may have a horoscope in a magazine which says that Mars is here or Jupiter is there, and that as a consequence this or that is likely to happen to you. Two questions immediately spring to mind: What do the planets signify? How does that affect an individual?

The theory is straightforward again, and not as complex as that of the zodiac signs in the previous chapter. Remember that the basic theory of astrology is that since the universe and mankind are part of the same Creation, they both move in a similar fashion, so Man's movements mirror those of the heavens. So far, so good. If you look at the sky, night after night, or indeed day after day, it looks pretty much the same; the stars don't move much in relationship to each other, at least not enough to notice. What do move, though, are the Sun and Moon, and five other points of light—the planets. It must therefore follow that if these are the things which move, they must be the things which can be related to the movements of Man. Perhaps, the theory goes, they have areas of the sky in which they feel more at home, where the energy that they represent is stronger; there might be other places where they are uncomfortable and weak, corresponding to the times in your life when you just can't win no matter what you do. The planets would then behave like ludo counters, moving round the heavens trying to get back to a home of their own colour, and then starting a new game.

The scheme sounds plausible, makes a sort of common sense, and is endearingly human; all hallmarks of astrological thought, which unlike scientific thought has to relate everything to the human experience. And so it is: the planets are given values to show the universal energy in different forms, and given signs of the zodiac as homes. Therefore your Sun sign also has a planet to look after it, and the nature of that planet will show itself strongly in your character.

The planets used are the Sun and Moon, which aren't really planets at all, one being a satellite and the other a star, and then Mercury, Venus, Mars, Jupiter, and Saturn. This was enough until the eighteenth century, when Uranus was discovered, followed in the subsequent two hundred years by Neptune and Pluto. Some modern astrologers put the three new planets into horoscopes, but it really isn't necessary, and may not be such a good idea anyway. There are three good reasons for this:

(a) The modern planets break up the symmetry of the original system, which was perfectly harmonious;

(b) The old system is still good enough to describe everything that can happen in a human life, and the modern planets have little to add;

(c) Astrology is about the relationship between the sky and a human being. An ordinary human being cannot see the outer planets on his own; he needs a telescope. We should leave out of the system such things as are of an extra-human scale or magnitude: they do not apply to an ordinary human. If we put in things which are beyond ordinary human capabilities, we cannot relate them to the human experience, and we are wasting our time.

In the diagram on page 21 the zodiac is presented in its usual form, but it has also been split into two from the start of Leo to the start of Aquarius. The right hand half is called the solar half, and the other one is the lunar half. The Sun is assigned to Leo because in the Northern hemisphere, where astrology started, August is when you feel the influence of the Sun most, especially in the Eastern Mediterranean, where the Greeks and the other early Western civilizations were busy putting the framework of astrology together in the second millennium BC. The Sun is important because it gives light. The Moon gives light too; it is reflected sunlight, but it is enough to see by, and this is enough to give the Sun and Moon the title of 'the Lights' in astrology. The Moon is assigned to Cancer, so that the two of them can balance and complement each other. From there, moving away from the Lights around the circle on both sides, the signs have the planets assigned to them starting with the fastest mover, Mercury, and continuing in decreasing order of speed. Saturn is the slowest mover of all, and the two signs opposite to

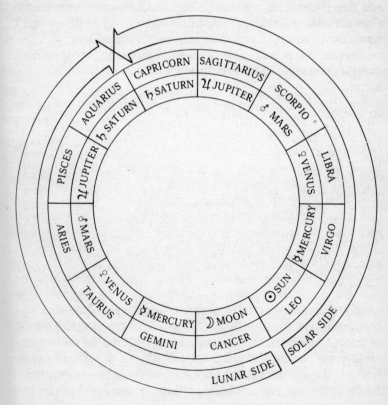

the Lights are both governed by that planet. The reasons for this apparent assymmetry will be explained in a little while. This arrangement is, of course, the horseshoe of the title to this chapter.

The Sun and Moon work in a similar fashion to the outgoing and collecting energies we noted earlier with the twelve signs. The Sun is radiant above all else; energy comes outwards from it, warming and energizing all those around it. Leo people, whose sign is the Sun's, work like this by being at the centre of a group of people and acting as inspiration and encouragement to them all. The Moon reflects the Sun's light, and energies of a lunar kind are directed inwards towards the core of the person. The two energies are necessarily linked; lunar people would starve without the solar folks' warmth, but the solar types need someone to radiate to or their purpose is unfulfilled.

The planets on each side of the horseshoe display their own energies in a solar or lunar way depending on which side of the pattern they are on.

Mercury and Venus form a pair, representing complementary but opposite ideas, which should be familiar by now. Mercury represents difference, and Venus stands for similarity.

Wherever anything new forms that is distinguishable from the background, then Mercury is there making it what it is, highlighting what makes it different. Anything separate is Mercurial, and words, since they are separate and can be strung together into millions of different combinations, are Mercurial too. Mercury is not a long-term influence; it notes things as being different for an instant, and then they become part of the establishment, and something else is new elsewhere. Because 'new' is an instantaneous state—that is, something can only be new once, and for a moment—Mercury is not associated with anything lasting, and its rapid motion as a planet leads to its being associated with the idea of speed. Virgo, Mercury's solar sign, is concerned with the changing of the shape of things ('collecting, using material' in our keyword system), while Gemini, the lunar sign, is concerned with reading and writing, and getting new ideas ('outgoing, using communication').

Venus does the reverse; it looks for that which is similar, finding points of contact to make relationships between common interests and energies. It likes to preserve the harmonies of life, and resents anything which might interrupt them. Love and affection are naturally Venusian, but so is music and all of the Arts, for the harmonies they contain. Expressed in a solar way, Venus is Libra, the maker of relationships; its lunar face is Taurus, emphasizing food and furnishings as things which give pleasure to the individual.

The next pair are Mars and Jupiter. Mars applies force from the outside to impose structure on a disordered universe, while Jupiter expands forcibly from the inside to give growth and wealth, inviting everyone else to join in.

Mars is pure force, energy in a straight line with a direction to go in. Anger and passion are both Martian, and so is lust, because they are all examples of great energy directed towards a given end. Note that Martian force is not necessarily strength, wealth, or know-how, just pure energy, which often boils over and needs controlling. Mars is the power in an athlete, and in an assassin too. It is also the power in a lover, because the urge to create is also the urge to pro-create, and if that energy fulfils its purpose then that creation takes place. Scorpio is its solar side, the power to control and create; in lunar form it is shown by Aries, as energy enjoyed for its own sake by its owner, with no purpose except to express it.

Jupiter is the spirit of expansion from within; not only does it oppose Mars' force from outside, it opposes Mars' physicality with its own mental emphasis. Jupiter develops the mind, then. As it does so, it develops all natural talents of an academic nature, and encourages movement, enquiry and travel to broaden experience and knowledge. The Solar expression of this is Sagittarius, where the centaur symbol is both a wise teacher and a free-roaming wild horse at the same time. Jupiter in a lunar sense is Pisces, where the imagination is developed to a greater extent than anywhere else, but used to provide an internal dream world for the owner's pleasure. Great sensitivity here, but the lunar energies are not of the sort to be expressed; rather other energies are *im*pressed on the Piscean mind.

Saturn is the last of the five planets. He stands alone, and if it is necessary to consider him as paired with anything it is with the Lights as an entity together. The Lights are at the centre of the system; Saturn is at its edge. They are the originators of the energies of the zodiac, and he is the terminator. Everything to do with limits and ends is his. He represents Time, and lots of it, in contrast to Mercury, which represented the instant. He represents the sum total of all things, and the great structures and frameworks of long-term endeavour. In solar form he is Capricorn, the representative of hard work, all hierarchies, and all rulers; in lunar form he is Aquarius, showing the horizontal structure of groups of people within society at different levels. Here he denies the activity of Mars, because society is too big for one person to change against the collective will, and he contains the expansion of Jupiter within himself. Venus and Mercury can neither relate to it nor make it change, because it is always the same, in the end.

The planets show important principles in action, the same as the zodiac does. You have probably noticed that the horseshoe of the planets and the ring of the zodiac say the same thing in a different way, and that is true about most things in astrology. It may be that the two systems interrelate and overlap because they are from the same source: after all, $3+2+2=7$, which is the planet's total, and $3\times2\times2=12$, which is the signs'. How you assign the elements and qualities, pairs of planets and lights is for you to decide. The joy of astrology, like all magic, is that it has you at the centre, and is made to fit its user's requirements. Now you know the principles, you can use it as you please, and as it seems relevant to you.

Part 2

Yourself—and Others

3. The Essential Leo

All the energy in the zodiac is solar, but that solar energy takes many forms. It is moderated and distributed through the planetary energies until it finally shows in you, the individual. As a Leo, there is no moderating planet in your case; you will be motivated by, and behave in the manner of, the energies of the Sun itself. To remind yourself of what that means, read pages 12 and 22 again. As a sign of the zodiac, Leo is a fixed Fire sign. Remind yourself what that means by reading page 13. Now we have to see how those essential principles work when expressed through a person and his motivation.

What it Means to be a Leo

You know what it is to be a Leo, because you are one; but you probably don't know what it is that makes a Leo the way he is, because you cannot stand outside yourself. You would have to be each of the other eleven signs in turn to understand the nature of the energy that motivates you. This essential energy is in every Leo, but it shows itself to different extents and in different ways. Because it is in every single Leo, it is universal rather than specific, and universal ideas tend to come in language which sounds a little on the woolly side. You will think that it isn't really about what makes you who you are, because you don't feel like that every day—or at least you think you don't. In fact, you feel like that all the time, but you don't notice it any more than you notice your eyes focusing, yet they do it all the time, and you see things the way you do because of it.

The first thing to note is that the zodiac is a circle, not a line with a beginning and an end. If it were a line, then Leo would be just over a third of the way along, but that would be to miss the point; if the zodiac is a circle, then Leo is a stage in an endlessly repeating cycle, and we will get a much better idea of what it is if we look to see where it came from, and where it is going.

The sign before Leo is Cancer. Cancer represents that stage of a person's existence where they want to be sure of themselves, and do everything possible for reassurance, or to guard their personal security. They feel that they are likely to be attacked, confronted, or asked to do impossible things at any moment, and they are sure that they will find such tasks beyond their capabilities. Only when the individual is quite secure in himself, and confident in his abilities, does the next phase begin; this is Leo.

Leo has the confidence in himself that the Cancerian lacks. He knows he can do things, and knows, too, that he is the best person to do them. He makes himself the centre of things, and makes sure everybody knows his position, then proceeds to play things his way.

The Leo phase is concerned with being in control, but also with being the instigator as well. It is the difference between being a commander and being a mere manager; words that imply a sense of action, command, and being the principal person are all Leonine in their feeling. Leos are kings, rulers, generals, emperors; they are leading lights, superstars, grandmasters, conductors of the orchestra. It is an essential part of the Leo experience to be addressed in terms of respect, using a title which shows recognition of the Leo's place at the centre of things.

The orchestral conductor is a particularly good example. The conductor is the one whose interpretation of the work is being expressed by the musicians. He organizes, leads, and conducts them, but he does none of the actual playing. He is seen as the focus of the performance: the applause is directed to, and received by, him. He inspires the performance; he is its originator, centre, and focus. What he does not do, however, is write the music (for this example, anyway) or play any of the instruments. Yet the players address him as 'Maestro', and his name is given billing of equal magnitude as that of the composer, if not more.

Why? Because he is taking the role of the Leo. He takes an existing situation (the music) and makes it his own. He is the heart of the performance. Energy radiates out from him as he inspires the other performers to work together in the expression of his vision of the music. Leos are always the inspiration of their group. They can put enthusiasm into others. They know it will all be worth it in the end. They have confidence in themselves, their abilities, and their vision.

The sheer radiance of a Leo's energy makes it difficult to see behind the source of the light: being dazzled is all too easy. Careful thought, though, shows up one or two things. Leos are quite confident about what they can do, but they are nothing like so confident about things that they haven't tried; this leads them to stick with the things they know well, and to dismiss new ideas as unimportant, as long as they think they can get away with it. As a Leo, you will have been enraged by the last sentence: how dare I suggest that there is anything you can't do! Everybody is wary of unfamiliar things, you will say. Not so: even among the other Fire signs, Sagittarius will try new things from pure curiosity, without thinking about whether he can succeed or not, while Aries will attempt anything at all, simply because the idea of not succeeding does not enter his head. *You* have to be sure that you will still be able to be the centre of appreciation after the event, and this makes you wary.

Still reading? I hope so. We both know that Leos are sensitive to being teased: the difference between us is that you don't tell everybody. The reason for this inflexibility of approach and avoidance of new adventures is that you are a Fixed sign. You have to maintain what you have, and to put your own energy out into your surroundings: in other words, you have to have life liveable *on your own terms*. You are doing this for yourself, in the only way you know how. It is not in your nature to do things for the benefit of others rather than yourself, and it is not in your power to change the nature of things through your own efforts. Both of these things you might like to do, and privately wish you could, but they are the province of the next sign on from yours, Virgo, and for the moment you must stay where you are. You cannot create things from your surroundings, you can only create things from yourself. When you create from yourself, you create an active force that others can use; they will do things for you, and then give you the credit for your inspiration and encouragement. You are the heart of their activity, and they do the circulating for you. Heart and circulation: a life-giving system together.

Leo corresponds to the heart in the body at all levels, from the individual to the collective. Your function in any group is to pump out inspiration and warmth; a group of people feels livelier, happier, and more active when you are at its heart. They have to do things at your rate, though; when someone challenges your authority, you cannot function. If you are rushed or flustered, you lose your power, and do odd things in an attempt to regain your rhythm. The last thing any group of people needs is a palpitating heart, or for some outsider to bring on a heart attack. No joke: all the 'heart' phrases apply to a Leo as he goes through life. You are naturally good-hearted and even great-hearted, but if there is nobody to receive your light and tell you how they appreciate you, you are down-hearted, faint-hearted, or even broken-hearted.

Leo is the sign of the Sun; like the Sun, you are a radiant centre to a whole system of satellites. People move around you, grateful for your stability and warmth. If you were to move or be displaced, the planets would be thrown out of orbit, and chaos would result. As you see, staying still and being warm is what you are best at.

Like the Sun, a Leo's essential function is to convert material resource into heat and light, and then to radiate this outwards.

This makes you a motivator of others; you supply that energy which others need to make things happen. You change things from a static state to an active one, and you place yourself at the centre of the activity.

This radiance of personal warmth gives you a reputation for generosity, which is true, but what the other eleven signs don't realize, especially the six 'collecting' signs (page 12), is that you can't help it. You can't *not* give out, in fact, which seems genuinely altruistic to others, because they have to get something in return if they are to give something out. What you do need, and they don't realize, is to be appreciated for the role you play at the centre of things. You know that when things aren't quite going your way you slip away and do something else to draw attention back to yourself; now you know why you do it. It's to re-establish yourself at the centre of things.

The rest of mankind is naturally attracted to your kind of warmth and light; without it the race would never continue. Literally, as it happens, because Leo is the sign given to the process of having chidren. The obstetric side of this is actually assigned to Cancer, but the child itself is Leo, because it represents a person's own energies put outside himself and made into physical form. The new individual can thus maintain (Fixed signs maintain, remember?) the activity (Fire sign) of his parent, and the line is extended for another generation.

Everything which is an expression of personal warmth is assigned to Leo. Children in all forms, not only the individuals, but also the processes of creating them, and all the happy and warm activities in life like love and laughter. Gambling is Leonine too, but only in that it is an extension of personal will in an attempt to influence chance. Wherever there is warmth and a feeling of wellbeing, wherever there is optimism and confidence, there is the spirit of Leo.

The lion of the sign is well chosen. Like the animal, Leo people are proud, confident, majestic, lazy, generous to their friends, and an inspiration to us all.

Early, Middle or Late? The Decanates

Each of the zodiac signs is divided into degrees, like an arch of any other circle. Since a circle has 360 degrees, then each sign must be 30 degrees, since there are twelve signs. Each of the signs is further split into sections of ten degrees, called decanates. There are three decanates in each sign, and the one that your birthday falls in will tell you a little more about how that Leonine energy actually works in you as an individual.

First decanate (23 July–1 August)
This is the purest form of Leo. There is a double helping of solar energy here, expressed without any other planet to give it shape or direction. This is pure radiance, where the energies of the person are used to glorify the self, and to write the joy of being a Leo large enough for the world to read it. There has to be one decanate of the thirty-six where the individual celebrates himself to the exclusion of everything else, and this is the one. The things attributed to this part of Leo are all things to be proud of: you probably find almost all of them to your taste. Children and births generally are here, because they are the pride of their parents, the joy of their family, and a Leo's creative ability made real. Here too is that other sort of child, the brainchild; it does not matter whether it is a novel, a painting, or just a good idea taken up and put into practice—each is a real thing born of the Leo's self-expression, reflecting his creative ability. Fashion and clothes are in this first decanate too, because they are an expression of the wearer and his personality. So is anything spectacular or showy; spontaneous displays of energy for their own sake are showing their solar side by giving out rather than taking in. Perhaps, on the human scale, you sometimes make grand gestures or give lavish parties just because you feel like it. And, of course, the heart of anything, whether literally or figuratively, belongs in this early third of Leo too.

Second decanate (2–11 August)
Here Jupiter adds its distinctive sense of size and humour. 'Jumbo' seems to be a good word for Jupiter: everything it touches is larger-than-life and fun. With Jupiter to moderate its radiance, the solar energy of the middle Leo is turned towards the intellectual and the spiritual. Education and school-days are given to this decanate sometimes; perhaps you enjoyed the cheeriness and the sense of all being best pals which never seems to be carried on into later life no matter how hard you try.

Jupiter has much to do with the good life: in this section of the sign the Leo is likely to enjoy good food and wine, and to see them as a natural expression of himself. Jupiter is also the alcohol in the wine, you see. The Sun and Jupiter together give an emphasis on 'good things gathered in': this can be natural produce like food and wines, but it can just as easily be profits from business, which will be displayed and enjoyed just as fully by the Leo in the form of the plush offices, big cars, expensive suits, and things like that which are an expression of a full and profitable life. The profits don't have to be earned, though; Jupiter is also the planet of strokes of sheer luck in return for trusting to fortune. Hunches which pay off, pools wins, successful days at the races are all part of this sector of the sign, and the Leos who receive the rewards offered to them usually enjoy them to the full. In short, this decanate is for people who not only enjoy the best that life has to offer, but who like to be seen to do so.

Third decanate (12–22 August)
The final decanate has Mars as its co-ruler; joined with the Sun as it is, the emphasis is on the physical expression of the self. Here are the Leos who like to take an active part in things, and of course like to win, as all Leos do. Not surprisingly, sport in all forms is assigned to this decanate. The ideas of asserting yourself in competition, showing the other players just what you can do, and winning, are very much of the flavour of the Sun with Mars. Military conquests are here, too: any wargamers amongst you?

Leos from this decanate are likely to draw attention to themselves with the sort of equipment they own—the best golf clubs, the fantastic car stereo with six speakers, the gold watch with a stopwatch and tachymeter. The emphasis is on performance where the previous decanate concentrated on luxury, but in both cases the idea is to express and draw attention to the owner's personality.

Mars has an almost infantile emotional quality to it at times, and a fierce passion, too: these last degrees of the sign give Leos who fall blindly and powerfully in love, giving everything in the hope of being recognized in their devotion by the object of their affections. This is as close as a Leo will get to the self-sacrifice which characterizes the next sign in the cycle, Virgo.

Three Phases of Life: Leo as Child, Adult, Parent

The Leo child

The Leo child is a boisterous creature, full of confidence and energy. He is often a little bigger, physically, than his classmates, and if he is allowed to indulge his hearty appetite to his heart's content, may well become rather too heavy for his age. Being big gains him the attention of the other children he mixes with, and he likes that: it is a habit that continues through life, and is the reason that many adult Leos are overweight.

If there is a position with a title attached to it the Leo child will make sure he gets it; the status of being Prefect or Year Captain appeals to him enormously. It is nothing to do with the responsibility of the post, but simply the status which goes with it. Similarly, if there is a school play or something similar, the Leo child will want to be the star—and will fill the role admirably if given the chance, for all Leos are at their best when there is an audience.

Generally speaking Leo children enjoy their childhood and schooldays very much indeed, probably because of the generally lively atmoshpere that most schools have. This is not so obvious a statement as you might think: Cancer and Capricorn children, for instance, treat school very seriously, and sometimes need reminding to smile occasionally. There are two things which the Leo child needs to learn in his early years which do not come easily to him at all, and any personal difficulties he has are usually due to one or the other of them. The first is that he has to realize he is not (except in very rare instances) the best scholar/athlete the world has ever seen: not being the best as a matter of course is hard on a young Leonine ego. The second is that respect is sometimes due to those in authority over him: Leos never really grasp the idea that respect is something given, not always received.

The Leo adult

The Leo adult has one immense advantage in life—it is almost impossible for anyone to dislike him. All the enthusiasm of his childhood is there, added to a generosity which seems to increase with age; even when he is being stubborn and refusing to see another point of view, he is a likeable, even lovable, character.

It is not the Fire-element side of Leo that causes any friction, it is the Fixed-quality side. Leos will have their own way at all costs, and they will not move from their position. The reasons for this are simple: the Leo genuinely believes that he knows best, and that the person most suited to do what he knows is right is himself. Anybody else must be misinformed, and there is no advantage in changing a system that works very well as it is. That, at least, is the explanation a Leo gives to himself. He is less likely to consider that adopting another person's viewpoint would move him away from the centre of activity, and divert attention from himself, but these are motives every bit as powerful as the ones he admits to, and possibly even more so.

There is a good side to this fixed-ness, of course; Leos have loyalty and stamina, of the sort which keeps them dedicated to the support of their dependants and the pursuit of their goals no matter what. They are not the sort of people who are interested in one thing one minute, and another the next.

Like all adults, Leos arrange their lives so that they can spend most of their time in a situation which is a comfortable outlet for their zodiacal energy.

This means that they fix things so that they are always at the centre of whatever is going on; so that they are always the focus of attention; so that they can be a source of creative ideas for everybody else; and so that this situation can continue. The disadvantages for the outsider are that other opinions are likely to be dismissed; that no real change in the situation is ever likely to take place; and that he is likely to find the Leo pompous and opinionated rather than warm and generous.

Forcing change on an adult Leo by changing things around him and then showing him how much he is out of touch with reality is very damaging to him. He can be deeply hurt by this, and the damage to the group from the resulting loss of warmth and goodwill makes it an exercise of dubious value.

The Leo parent

Leo parents have one great talent, and one great disadvantage. The great talent is the love, warmth and generosity that flows freely from all Leos, and which is especially true in the case of their own offspring. No child of Leo parents ever suffers from not being loved and cherished. A Leo parent identifies with his child to an extent not found in many of the other signs—he can remember what it is to be a child, and enjoy his child's little triumphs and catastrophes with all the vividness of the child's imagination.

The big disadvantage is that he may be too imposing and demanding. Leos are proud of their children, and want their children to be a credit to them. They want their friends to admire their children as an extension of their Leonine selves, which they are, of course. Children, however, are rarely the paragons required for this sort of activity, and the result is that the Leonine parent becomes over-corrective of minor behaviour faults in the child, seeing them as affronts to his own self-respect.

Leo parents are dominant in their own homes; they 'rule' them like the kings the sign represents. They decide who does what, and this can mean that a child is forced to pursue some activity which the Leo parent thinks would be good for him, but in which the child has little interest. Children are individuals, and must develop their individuality; but if they have Leo parents they must recognize that it is the Leo who is the dominant personality in the household, and they may have to wait until they leave home before they can develop their own interests and talents.

4. Leo Relationships

How Zodiacal Relationships Work

You might think that relationships between two people, described in terms of their zodiac signs, might come in 144 varieties; that is, twelve possible partners for each of the twelve signs. The whole business is a lot simpler than that. There are only seven varieties of relationship, although each of those has two people in it, of course, and the role you play depends on which end of the relationship you are at.

You may well have read before about how you are supposed to be suited to one particular sign or another. The truth is usually different. Leos are supposed to get on with Arians and Sagittarians, and indeed they do, for the most part, but it is no use reading that if you have always found yourself attracted to Pisceans, is it? There has to be a reason why you keep finding Pisceans attractive, and it is not always to do with your Sun sign; other factors in your horoscope will have a lot to do with it. The reason you prefer people of certain signs as friends or partners is because the relationship of your sign to theirs produces the sort of qualities you are looking for, the sort of behaviour you find satisfactory. When you have identified which of the seven types of basic relationship it is, you can see which signs will produce that along with your own, and then read the motivation behind it explained later on in more detail in 'The Leo Approach to Relationships' and the individual compatibility sections.

Look at the diagram on page 16. All you have to do is see how far away from you round the zodiacal circle your partner's Sun sign is. If they are Capricorn, they are five signs in front of you. You are also, of course, five signs behind them, which is also important, as you will see in a little while. If they are Taurus, they are three signs behind you, and you are three signs in front of them. There are seven possibilities: you can be anything up to six signs apart, or you can both be of the same sign.

Same sign

Somebody who is of the same sign as you acts in the same way that you do, and is trying to achieve the same result for himself. If your goals permit two winners, this is fine, but if only one of you can be on top, you will argue. No matter how temperamental, stubborn, devious, or critical you can be, they can be just the same, and it may not be possible for you to take the same kind of punishment you hand out to others. In addition, they will display every quality which really annoys you about yourself, so that you are constantly reminded of it in yourself as well as in them. Essentially, you are fighting for the same space, and the amount of tolerance you have is the determining factor in the survival of this relationship.

One sign apart

Someone one sign forward from you acts as an environment for you to grow in. In time, you will take on those qualities yourself. When you have new ideas, they can often provide the encouragement to put them into practice, and seem to have all your requirements easily available. Often, it is this feeling that they already know all the pitfalls that you are struggling over which can be annoying; they always seem to be one step ahead of you, and can seemingly do without effort all the things which you have to sweat to achieve. If the relationship works well, they are helpful to you, but there can be bitterness and jealousy if it doesn't.

Someone one sign back from you can act as a retreat from the pressures of the world. They seem to understand your particular needs for rest and recovery, whatever they may be, and can usually provide them. They can hold and understand your innermost secrets and fears; indeed, their mind works best with the things you fear most, and the fact that they can handle these so easily is a great help to you. If the relationship is going through a bad patch, their role as controller of your fears gets worrying, and you will feel unnerved in their presence, as though they were in control of you. When things are good, you feel secure with them behind you.

Two signs apart
Someone two signs forward from you acts like a brother or sister. They are great friends, and you feel equals in each other's company; there is no hint of the parent-child or master-servant relationship. They encourage you to talk, even if you are reticent in most other company; the most frequently heard description of these relationships is 'We make each other laugh'. Such a partner can always help you put into words the things that you want to say, and is there to help you say them. This is the relationship that teenagers enjoy with their 'best friend'. There is love, but it does not usually take sexual form, because both partners know that it would spoil the relationship by adding an element of unnecessary depth and weight.

Someone two signs behind you is a good friend and companion, but not as intimate as somebody two signs forward. They are the sort of people you love to meet socially; they are reliable and honest, but not so close that things become suffocatingly intense. They stop you getting too serious about life, and turn your thoughts outwards instead of inwards, involving you with other people. They stop you from being too selfish, and help you give the best of yourself to others. This relationship, then, has a cool end and a warm end; the leading sign feels much closer to his partner than the trailing sign does, but they are both satisfied by the relationship. They particularly value its chatty quality, the fact that it works even better when in a group, and its tone of affection and endearment rather than passion and obsession.

Three signs apart

Someone three signs in front of you represents a challenge of some kind or another. The energies of the pair of you can never run parallel, and so must meet at some time or another. Not head on, but across each other, and out of this you can both make something strong and well established which will serve the two of you as a firm base for the future. You will be surprised to find how fiercely this person will fight on your behalf, or for your protection; you may not think you need it, and you will be surprised that anybody would think of doing it, but it is so nonetheless.

Someone three signs behind you is also a challenge, and for the same reasons as stated above; from this end of the relationship, though, they will help you achieve the very best you are capable of in a material sense. They will see to it that you receive all the credit that is due to you for your efforts, and that everyone thinks well of you. Your reputation is their business, and they will do things with it that you could never manage yourself. It's like having your own P.R. team. This relationship works hard, gets results, and makes sure the world knows it. It also looks after itself, but it needs a lot of effort putting in.

Four signs apart

Someone four signs forward from you is the expression of yourself. All the things you wanted to be, however daring, witty, sexy, or whatever, they already are, and you can watch them doing it. They can also help you to be these things. They do things which you think are risky, and seem to get away with them. There are things you aim towards, sometimes a way of life that you would like to have, which these people seem to be able to live all the time; it doesn't seem to worry them that things might go wrong. There are lots of things in their life which frighten you, which you would lie awake at nights worrying about, which they accept with a child's trust, and which never go wrong for them. You wish you could be like that.

Someone four signs behind you is an inspiration to you. All the things you wish you knew, they know already. They seem so wise and experienced, and you feel such an amateur; luckily, they are kind and caring teachers. They are convincing, too. When they speak, you listen and believe. It's nice to know there's somebody there with all the answers. This extraordinary relationship often functions as a mutual admiration society, with each end wishing it could be more like the other; unfortunately, it is far less productive than the three-sign separation, and much of its promise remains unfulfilled. Laziness is one of the inherent qualities of a four-sign separation; all its energies are fulfilled, and it rarely looks outside itself for something to act upon. Perhaps this is just as well for the rest of us.

Five signs apart
Someone five signs ahead of you is your technique. You know what you want to do; this person knows how to do it. He can find ways and means for you to do what you want to be involved in, and he can watch you while you learn and correct your mistakes. They know the right way to go about things, and have the clarity of thought and analytical approach necessary if you are to get things clear in your mind before you get started

Someone five signs behind you is your resource. Whenever you run out of impetus or energy, they step forward and support you. When you're broke, they lend you money, and seldom want it returned. When you need a steadying hand because you think you've over-reached yourself, they provide it. All this they do because they know that it's in their best interest as well as yours, to help you do things, and to provide the material for you to work with. You can always rely on them for help, and it's nice to know they will always be there. They cannot use all their talent on their own; they need you to show them how it should be done. Between you, you will use all that you both have to offer effectively and fully, but it is a relationship of cooperation and giving; not all the zodiac signs can make it work well enough.

Six signs apart
Someone six signs apart from you, either forwards or backwards, is both opponent and partner at the same time. You are both

essentially concerned with the same area of life, and have the same priorities. Yet you both approach your common interests from opposite directions, and hope to use them in opposite ways. Where one is private, the other is public, and where one is self-centred, the other shares himself cheerfully. The failings in your own make-up are complemented by the strengths in the other; it is as if, between you, you make one whole person with a complete set of talents and capabilities. The problem with this partnership is that your complementary talents focus the pair of you on a single area of life, and this makes for not only a narrow outlook, but also a lack of flexibility in your response to changes. If the two of you are seeing everything in terms of career, or property, or personal freedom, or whatever, then you will have no way to deal effectively with a situation which cannot be dealt with in those terms. Life becomes like a seesaw; it alternates which end it has up or down, and can sometimes stay in balance; but it cannot swing round to face another way, and it is fixed to the ground so that it does not move.

These are the only combinations available, and all partnerships between two people can be described as a version of one of the seven types. It must be remembered, though, that some of the roles engendered by these dispositions of sign to sign are almost impossible to fulfil for some of the signs, because their essential energies, and the directions they are forced to take by the planets behind them, drive them in ways which make it too difficult. To form a relationship based on sharing and acceptance is one thing: to do it when you are governed by a planet like Mars is somethings else. Even when the relationship can form, the sort of approach produced by, say, Jupiter, is a very different thing from that produced by Venus.

The next thing you must consider, then, is how you, as a Leo, attempt relationships as a whole, and what you try to find in them. Then you must lay the qualities and outlook of each of the twelve signs over the roles they must play in the seven relationship types, and see whether the pair of you manage to make the best of that relationship, or not.

The seven relationship types are common to all the signs,

relating to all the other signs. You can use your understanding of them to analyse and understand the relationship between any pair of people that you know, whether or not they are Leonine; but to see how the characters fit into the framework in more detail, you will need to look at the individual compatibilities, of which just the Leo ones are given in this book.

The Leo Approach to Relationships

Not all Leos actually want, or need, a close one-to-one relationship which will last them all their lives. It would be a very rare person indeed who could adequately receive and reflect all the light and heat a Leo has to offer; very often that purpose is best served by a whole range of people—an audience, in fact.

Nor does a Leo ever really need a soul-mate in the same way as, for instance, a Libran does. Leos are quite capable of looking after themselves, and they don't feel left out or isolated by the feeling that nobody else is quite the same as they are; in fact, it reinforces their view that they are indeed rather special, something out of the ordinary. Many Leos are open and social on the surface, but rather withdrawn inside: it takes an unusually persistent person to attempt to look behind the brilliance and the warmth, and the Leo is not likely to thank them for doing so.

The essence of the thing is that Leos are people who exist on their own rather than in groups. There is no point in a Leo being like everybody else, or in finding somebody just like himself to be friends with: to do such a thing would destroy his sense of his own uniqueness. He needs an adoring public, and he needs friends, but he does not necessarily need a confidant or a comforter—those things he can do for himself. After all, if you are right all the time, and always get your own way, why do you need to confide in people, and when are you ever miserable?

There is a handy astrological reminder for this description of the inner Leo, and it has to do with the planetary adjectives. Jupiter's people are jovial, Saturn's people are saturnine, and so on. Leo is ruled by the Sun, and its people are . . . solitary.

When a Leo does enter a relationship with somebody, no matter how deep he intends the relationship to become, he approaches it in the same way. He has certain expectations, certain things to offer, and wants certain things in return. What he wants to do is to direct his light, warmth, love, generosity, in fact the full force of his personality radiated outwards, onto the other person. This makes them feel very special; they are made to feel as though all the good things there are in the world are happening to them at once. The Leo wants to elevate his new friend to the status of being an honorary Leo, so that they can know what fun it is to enjoy the best of life all the time.

In return he wants to be adored. Leos go through life saying, in effect, 'Look how wonderful I am to you', but a *relationship* is formed when the other person replies, 'Gosh, you're so wonderful to me'. It's not a bad way of doing things, even if it sounds a little off-putting, especially to Aquarians (who naturally represent the opposite point of view). The Leo has energy to spare, and is giving it out anyway; the partner might as well be on the receiving end of it as anyone else. This is a simple thing, which non-Fire-signs never grasp: the energy comes free—you don't have to pay for it. Water signs in particular find this impossible to understand. If the partner is then appreciative of what he gets from the Leo, the Leo's happiness is complete. He gets gratitude, in effect, just for being himself. How could anything be better?

What a Leo doesn't want out of a relationship is for his actions to be criticized. He does things in the way he thinks is best, and if the partner attempts to change or reject what he is doing, then that shows that the Leo must be, in the partner's eyes, wrong in some way. Leos are hurt by this. They do things to make people happy, and everybody has a good time whenever they are around, and then somebody dares to say that he should be doing things a different way! The Leonine display of disapproval is usually in the form of accusations of *lèse-majesté*, but beneath the regal exterior lies a deeply wounded soul. He will not forget—an attempt has been made to extinguish his light, and it will take time for him to return to his full heat and brilliance again.

In friendships, Leos are wonderfully warm. If you are appreciative of their talents, they are almost endlessly generous, and it is not necessary for the friend to attempt to reciprocate on the same scale—the Leo enjoys treating his friends. Because friendships do not necessarily have to be intimate, the Leo can remain 'solitary' within the framework of the friendship, doing what he does best and being appreciated for it. Leos have lots of friendships like this, and it is where they work best.

In love affairs, Leos are powerful and ardent lovers—what else would you expect from the heat of a Fire sign and the weight of a Fixed sign? They are constant in love—the Fixed-ness again—and are not therefore likely to change partners for its own sake. Because they are not fickle or flighty in themselves, they are easily wounded by partners who are, seeing the apparent change in affection as a criticism of themselves. It is not a situation that happens a great deal, though; few people want to trade the luxury of an affair with a Leo for anything else unless the affair is completely unworkable. And having an affair with a Leo is indeed a life of luxury; he will expect you to join him in as high a lifestyle as you can both manage. This is not a relationship where you live in romantic poverty with each other.

In marriage, Leos have to make a few compromises. In practice this means that they learn how to be themselves in ways which do not actually have their partner on the verge of tears, because they are not used to making allowances for other people. It is really a lot easier all round if the partner just agrees to do things in the Leo's way after all. Whichever partner is the Leo, then they will be the dominant force in the marriage, especially if the other partner is neither Fixed nor Fire. It is sometimes better this way, though the other partner must be prepared to take the minor role. There is no doubt that the Leo loves his partner dearly, and will show this all the time, but he will naturally expect to be the decision-maker. He does not naturally expect to be the person who does all the work which follows on from the decisions he has taken, though, and this can sometimes lead to one or two cross words. In the end, the partner will have to let him have his way, and will be rewarded with a lasting and affectionate marriage, a high standard of living, and a warm family life. It sounds like a good deal.

Individual Compatibilities Sign by Sign

All relationships between the signs work in the ways described earlier in 'How Zodiacal Relationships Work' (page 37). In addition to that, descriptions of how a Leo attempts to form a relationship with someone from each of the twelve signs are given below. I have tried to show not what a Libran, for example, is like, but what a Leo sees him as, and how he sees you. Each individual Libran looks different, of course, but their motivation is the same, and these descriptions are meant to help you understand what you re trying to do with them, and how they are trying to handle you. As usual, the words he and his can be taken to mean she and her, since astrology makes no distinction here.

Leo-Aries

This is one of the great friendships of the zodiac. You think that they are dynamic and confident, just the way you think people should be, but they change direction too much for your taste: they will no doubt settle down in a few years' time. They think that you have the right sort of enthusiasm but you are a little unadventurous, a bit of a home-lover, in their eyes; all you need is a bit of a push and you will be on the right track. How much you are going to enjoy trying to make these final adjustments in each other!

Of course, neither of you will succeed in making the other more like yourself, and it is better that you should not succeed anyway. The little differences give that extra sparkle to the relationship and stop it from becoming boring.

You do have a great amount in common. Both of you are Fire signs; both of you believe that action is better than inaction, that getting personally involved is the only way to be effective, and that your own ideas are naturally the best ones available. People who sit still, or particularly who worry about things, bore both of you very quickly—you are both optimistic and forward looking, confident that you can handle anything that comes your way.

Examine that last phrase again. Leos are not normally confident about handling new things; familiar things, yes, but not new ones. Where has the confidence come from? From Aries: to you he represents the source of all personal energy. You are always bothered that you might not have the resources to cope with anything completely new and unfamiliar, in case it requires more than you've got; Aries seems to be an inexhaustible supply of whatever it takes, and your confidence in facing the unfamiliar grows strong in his company. After all, you think, between us we must have more than enough energy for anything, and you are right.

It works the other way round, too: Aries knows that he has the raw bravery to attack anything that comes his way, but he also knows that he doesn't have the staying power of the Leo. If a problem is likely to withstand his first onslaught and require real determination to overcome, then he knows he would be better off trying something else, and changes direction accordingly. A partnership with Leo gives him the stamina he didn't have before, and he is the stronger and more capable for it.

In terms of their element, Fire, Arians always had the spark of ignition, but didn't have the heat of combustion. Together, the two signs give a steady burning fire which can be started anywhere.

In a friendship, the thing you will like about each other most is the fact that you are each as enthusiastic and energetic as the other. The Arian doesn't have to slow down and wait for the Leo, or limit his activity in any way, nor does the Leo find the Arian too cautious to share fully in his grandiose way of life. Both of you find life exciting, and you find plenty to make you smile; you are used to things going right, and used to feeling pleased with yourselves. To have a friend who feels exactly the same way is very satisfying indeed.

In love, you both bring the heat of your Fire sign energies along with you, and your physical relationship is likely to be both hot and strong. It is not that you are not romantic, but underneath the sentiment you are both essentially interested in expressing your energy through physical activity. Neither of you wants to take from the other—you are both givers, and with such generous contributions from both sides you are going to have a fine time. Enthusiasm and confidence make for more of the same: you can't lose. The only way in which you are different is that the Arian is likely to tire of the relationship before you. He is not necessarily exhausted, but he needs fresh challenges to be at his best, and too much that is too familiar makes him restless.

As a marriage or as business partners you should work very well indeed. If you try to dominate the Arian he will direct his energies elsewhere, which would be detrimental to the partnership, so try not to organize him overmuch. The only other problem is that you both like spending money more than you like saving it: somebody has got to keep an eye on the finances.

Leo-Taurus

This is what you could call a steady relationship. If you are the sort of Leo whose energies are best directed into material things, who dines well and has a sumptuously decorated house, then this is the relationship for you.

It is an accumulating partnership: almost from the word go you will find yourselves buying things together that somehow express the pleasure you get from each other's company. Most of these things will be expensive, luxury items that appeal to you both. Perhaps you will be surprised at how your tastes coincide: in fact they don't, but they overlap quite substantially in the realms of the opulent and ostentatious. As the relationship goes on, you will find that you have collected a large number of things together—the relationship is taking visible form as these objects.

It is a relationship where the essential principle is strength and position. The maintenance of your position is vital to both of you, and in many ways this partnership over-emphasizes the heavier facets of your personalities at the expense of the others. The Taurean's gentleness and feeling for the land will not be in evidence when in your company, and your generosity to others will be diminished in the same way.

What the Taurean is after is material security; he measures his existence by his surroundings, and the more things he can touch and keep, then the better he feels. Your way of life usually involves any number of nice objects as a matter of course, and the Taurean finds these very attractive. You are naturally generous, and will probably take your Taurean to a restaurant soon after your initial meeting, or give them a small present. They will be highly appreciative; material things are important to them, and they keep them for ever. You enjoy being appreciated, and you enjoy being generous, because it expresses your confidence and your liking for yourself. They enjoy being taken out, and love receiving presents, because it increases their liking for *them*selves. You have found the perfect receptacle for your generosity, and it will all be converted into material form.

What you want is simply someone to appreciate you, and you will certainly have that in the Taurean: the problems arise when you start to get what you *don't* want. You don't want someone who is not going to do things your way, and you don't want someone who is going to stand his ground when you are trying to move him. Taureans do exactly this. You have two alternatives: either you can both stand your ground and shout at each other, which is quite likely, and not very productive, since at the end of the day you will have to move because they will outlast you (a Taurean will stay in the same position until he dies, if need be); or you can take their point of view and bring your own special radiance to it, which is the likely result. You can now see why you are accumulating so many expensive things: they are 'Leonized' Taurean acquisitions.

As friends, you will enjoy the good things of life together. Provided that you live essentially separate lives, you are unlikely to quarrel, and the biggest problem that faces you is that of obesity, since you encourage each other's over-consumption in all senses.

As lovers you will be powerful but rather ponderous in your behaviour. There is no sparkle to the union, and it degenerates into a power game before long. You are both possessive, and this could slow things down further.

Provided that you don't spend too much time fighting each other from entrenched positions, both marriage or a business relationship would work well. Money is an essential lubricant in this relationship though, and if there isn't enough of it, things will stop moving very quickly.

Leo-Gemini

There could hardly be a greater contrast between two partners than there is between the Taurean and the Gemini. The last one was a rather static and materialistic partnership, but this one is bright, alive, and fun all the way.

Gemini doesn't care how much money you have, or how generous you are. What he cares about most of all is how much joy you get out of being yourself: he has a similar feeling about himself, and he can't wait to share it with you, and to find out about your feelings at the same time.

You see him as the sort of friend you always wanted: bright, pleased to see you, actively seeking your company, and making you feel part of whatever he's doing. You love a chance to show yourself off: there is always some way to do that in a Gemini's company. You don't like dull surroundings: there is always something lively happening wherever a Gemini is, and he always regards it as a bit of a game, something diverting and not to be taken seriously. How could you not shine in an atmosphere like this? All the ponderous and static parts of your nature are miraculously converted into good-humoured boisterousness by the Mercurial talents of the Gemini. You can't stand still for too long when he's around, but he has taken away your fear of having to try unfamiliar things by doing them for you—you stay where you are in the midst of all the fun while he presents new things to you for your amusement in a constant stream. In many ways the relationship is like that between a king and his jester. He is a willing satellite, racing around you at a giddy rate while you stay beaming in the centre, and you find the arrangement very satisfying.

He sees you as somebody he can rely on. You are always going to be constant in your reactions to him, and he finds this useful.

He may change his tune from one minute to the next, and he knows it full well, but to have a friend who finds him fascinating no matter which side out he is, and who will always be there, is something worth looking after. He is also well aware of the fact that he needs shelter and support from time to time when one or another of his schemes collapses; Geminis are very good talkers, but their lives seldom match their plans. In such cases it is most reassuring to have a friend who will stick up for you, not betray you, and lend you a few quid when you're broke—a sort of ersatz elder brother. Leo fulfils this role for Gemini admirably, and the Gemini loves it. It's not all take and no give, though: the Gemini can, and does, render the Leo worthwhile service. It works like this: a Leo likes to know what's going on in the world, to be up to date, so that he can stay in command. If he is overtaken by new developments, then he could be made to look silly, and this he is anxious to avoid. Finding out about things from ground level is a bit undignified for a regal Lion, so he gets his information off the Gemini, who picks up information like the rest of us breathe— regularly, without thinking about it. It looks like the king and his jester again.

As a friendship, this has everything to recommend it. You, Leo, have to accept that the Gemini will tell you different tales on different days, and you mustn't expect him to give you much in the way of respect. He does like you a lot, though: he relies on you, in fact, as much as a Gemini relies on anybody.

As lovers, you are more likely to break ribs from laughter than from the fierceness of your embrace. The light, playful, essentially un-serious way a Gemini leads his public life extends to his private life as well. The Leo must remember that the Gemini has no real notion of loyalty or commitment, but provided he can live with that, the two of you can have a wonderful time playing expensive and intimate charades with each other.

For business, the combination could hardly be bettered. Your unity of purpose but difference of approach will have your competitors absolutely baffled.

For marriage, and especially for family life, these two signs have a lot to offer each other. Leo gives the warmth to sustain a long relationship, and Gemini stops it from becoming too set in its ways.

Leo-Cancer
The relationships formed with the sign immediately before or after your own are the most difficult of all; to give you your due, you manage this difficult task better than the other eleven signs, but you are still unlikely to choose a partner from a sign adjacent to your own unless other factors in your horoscope predispose you to do so. The reason is simple: the sign before your own represents you looking over your own shoulder. All the things you would rather not think about, they embody.

You see a Cancerian as an impossibly worried person; how, you think, could anyone be so afraid of life as they are? How do they manage to get up in the morning? The answer is through familiar and safe routines, and with care, not at all like your confident stride through life, trusting in Fortune to smile on you. The pair of you have very, very different views on life. You give them everything, and they seem to offer you nothing in return. You wear your heart on your sleeve, but you know next to nothing about how they feel. Worse yet, they don't tell you how much they appreciate you.

It's not as bad as it seems, though you will have to try very hard to see it the way it really is. They are actually in awe of your energy and generosity. A Cancer assimilates things a bit at a time, making sure they are thoroughly familiar before moving on to the next section; the scope and power of your way of doing things, in great open gestures, is too much for them to handle all at once. You are also very loud and open when you speak; they are very shy. If they could manage to answer you in the way you expect, you would probably do something else large and dramatic by way of response, and that would be altogether too much for them to manage. Quite simply, you overwhelm them.

Cancer would like to show you how much you are appreciated, and this is done by caring for you when you are not feeling as brilliant as usual. There is no such time, you cry, and there may well not be. Even if there were, your solar, solitary nature would prevent you from either taking or seeking comfort from another, and so the Cancerian's prime function is denied. You really aren't a great deal of use to each other—one is too much for the other to handle, the other offers a response that the first one doesn't want.

There is a subtler way, too, in which the Cancerian gives you all the things you don't want. As you know, you feel confident about yourself because you have mastered your fears about yourself fairly early on in life: they only come to the surface again when you are presented with something completely new. Changing circumstances worry you, because you will have to make yourself master of them before you can settle back into the role of the relaxed, unflappable, serene, ruling figure. For this reason you are none too fond of practical jokes: you laugh because you feel you have to, but you are seething inside because somebody has tried to unsettle your confidence. Inside every Leo there is a worried person, but he is a very long way down inside, and he need not be considered most of the time. A Cancerian brings him to you in the form of another individual; just as worried, just as defensive, just as easily upset. In fact a Cancerian is much more than these, and works on a different wavelength altogether, but you don't see that—all you see is the parts of yourself you'd rather not remember.

It is difficult to make this friendship really work; you really can't function with someone who worries every time you get interested in something, and they just can't stand the tension—they think your luck's got to give out sometime.

It is unlikely that you will be lovers, at least on the level of your Sun-sign energies: if you are, though, you will find that the major stumbling block is their inability to really *give* themselves. Keep the relationship lighter if you really want to keep it going—both of you enjoy the surface of courtship, with the flowers and the candlelit dinners, so leave it there.

As a marriage you can only make this partnership work if you adopt very traditional mother and father roles, and stick rigidly to them. The Leo is the father, the Cancer the mother, of course. A more modern or loosely structured relationship will probably not work.

Leo-Leo

Forming a partnership of any kind with a person of the same sign as yourself is not always a good thing, but on the other hand it is nowhere near the disaster it is sometimes made out to be. At least you know what you're getting!

Here the relationship is made from two people who both like being the centre of attention, and both like having a good time. The easiest way to make this work is to avoid any sort of situation where either of you have to make a decision—each of you would like to be the one to do it, and neither of you will be particularly keen to do what the other has decided. If you are simply enjoying each other's company in an environment where the rules for behaviour are well known and familiar, then you will have no problems at all; everybody else in the immediate area will find themselves being naturally drawn to the crackle of energy between you, and before you know where you are there will be a spontaneous party.

What you like about another Leo is their openness and optimism. There is nothing secretive about a Leo, for he has no need to be. When one Leo meets another, they both feel very relaxed, because they each know that the other is not trying to manoeuvre him in some sort of personal chess game the way the Scorpio does, or use Leonine energy to meet his own needs, as the Taurean sometimes does. Openness leads to trust and confidence, and confidence to radiance as the Leonine solar energy starts to make itself felt; the situation becomes an improving circle, as each partner makes the other feel good.

A Leo puts out solar energy, and likes to see some of it reflected back to him by appreciative friends. This energy usually returns in a much weaker form than what it went out as. When the appreciative friend is another Leo, the energy comes back full strength, and the pair of them can literally bask in each other's warmth.

Similar openness; similar radiance. The combination looks very positive until you remember that only one of you can be the dominant partner, but that both of you have a real need to dominate. Once one of you is established as the dominant partner, the other one must do one of only three things: he could displace you, and be dominant himself; he could go somewhere else and become the centre of a new group; or he could stay in your shadow, which would lead to much frustration, and eventually illness. As you can see, all three lead to the dissolution of the partnership: the obvious conclusion to be drawn is that if the relationship is to survive, then neither of you must be the dominant partner. The only way to implement this is for you to take turns. Since you are Fixed signs, you have a natural reluctance to changing roles more often than you have to, and you are much better off in one position over a long period of time. The best compromise seems to be to divide your areas of responsibility between you, and for each of you to take absolute responsibility for your own areas. Stay inside your own territory for things which matter, but share the limelight for the lighter and more social side of life, where you are not so likely to be fighting for position. In some ways it is an artificial answer, but it is the only workable one. Remember that those star systems with two suns have them revolving about each other, sharing responsibility for their satellites; they cannot work any other way.

As a light friendship the Leo-Leo pairing is a lot of fun. When the friendship becomes an affair, then the gestures become even grander until one of you feels that the other is taking too much of a controlling interest. Then you will disengage with polite dignity, maintaining as much of your self-respect as possible, and quietly look for someone more suitable.

As a marriage, you should work very well provided you do not try to control each other. You both have expansive ideas and the enthusiasm to match; given time, you will be able to achieve almost everything you set out to.

Leo-Virgo

This is the second of the adjacent-sign relationships open to you, and it is no easier than the last one, though you may take some small comfort from the fact that from the Virgo's point of view it is even more impossible than from yours. Oddly enough, this one works very well as a business partnership, because you have all the expansive ideas and the Virgo looks for ways to put them into practice in the most effective and economical way. You provide the fuel for him to work with, and give him the enthusiasm and breadth of outlook he needs to succeed.

On a personal level, though, the partnership is not so cosy. A Virgo has a need to examine things at a very close and fine level; unless he is familiar with the detail of things he is not happy. Broad concepts have no meaning for him; he can only take things in by building a large picture from many small ones. He tends to look down rather than up or outwards, and his attention is focused on the actual workings of things rather than how they look or what they mean.

You will be able to see at once that his insistence on understanding the detail of things will lead to difficulty when he examines much of your behaviour, where the detail is missing altogether. You start at the top and often neglect the smaller details; they are not important to your scheme of things. Worse still, you are concerned with ideas and activity rather than actual material articles. How can there be any real communication between you if you deal in different universes and on a different scale?

Obviously what communication actually takes place is going to be misinterpreted, and that's what happens. To you, the Virgo is always picking holes in your arguments, pointing out inconsistencies or impracticalities, and generally acting like a wet blanket. This is not actually true, but it's how it seems to you. What is happening is that the poor Virgoan is genuinely trying to understand what you are saying, but he can only do it by building up a picture a piece at a time, like a jigsaw. If there aren't enough pieces, or if a piece is missing, or the pattern changes, he complains; and there you are trying to get him to do his own painting with a broad brush.

He appreciates your energy, the same as everybody else, but he can't get over your apparent sloppiness. I know that you're generous and expansive rather than sloppy, but to the Virgoan it seems that way. He does things again and again, building up familiarity through practice, but you prefer to let someone else do that sort of thing, and he can't understand how you could possibly think that way. It's not that you are different—it's that neither of you can see what the other is trying to do, and are thus unable to communicate.

As friends you stand no real chance unless you can find some common interest which will allow you each to see what the other is doing; as business partners, though, you would do very well, as mentioned earlier.

If you want a Virgo as a lover you will have to be very patient and try to do things on a small scale. They don't appreciate your theatrical gestures—firstly because they are rather shy and restrained emotionally, and secondly because unless the intention is matched by something material, they won't be able to understand it. They will appreciate your warmth, though, and will repay you by doing all they can to please you—a show of appreciation which will do much to win your heart.

For a marriage, there are vast differences in outlook to be overcome. You may not be able to stand the Virgo's narrow point of view, and even if your optimism cures their constant worries, they may not be able to join you in your grand schemes as you would wish.

Leo-Libra

Librans are supposed to be the nicest people in the zodiac. To an extent it is true, but it depends an awful lot on your definition of nice. You will find them delightful company, but they are a little on the lightweight side when it comes to making firm moves. As long as you are prepared to provide the motive power for both of you, this partnership can be very rewarding.

A Libran sees you as the personification of his ambitions. Put simply, he would like to be like you. He is outgoing and sociable in the same way that you are, putting his energy out into friendly chat. He makes friends with everybody he meets; everybody likes a Libran. A lot of this is to do with the way his planet, Venus, works: Venus looks for something similar to itself all the time, and needs something to relate to. A Libran finds something to like about everybody he meets, something in the other person which is similar to something in himself. Then he talks about how similar he is to the other person, and how he has always liked being like this or like that. It's a sure-fire way of making people like you, but it's not a deliberate device, any more than you are generous for a reason: it's just the planet behind the person making all the moves in accordance with its nature. A Libran is the original source of communication between people, and of the relationship that brings into being. He is also the source of all that is harmonious, balanced or beautiful, because his insistence on drawing together those things which are similar eliminates contrast, disagreement and imbalance. It is not difficult to see why they have a reputation for being nice.

The trouble with being nice is that nobody thinks you are important or effective. We only sit up and take notice of things that stand out from, or disrupt, our previous steady state. Leos, now, they're different. When a Leo walks into a room the room sits up expectantly, and when he speaks everybody listens. A Libran would love to have that kind of effect on people. It's not the confidence he lacks, it's the effectiveness.

That's one of the things that attracts him to you: the other is that you generally get what you want, and live in a fairly wealthy way, compared to the rest of your friends. Librans would like to own all sorts of beautiful things, and live very elegant lifestyles to go with them, but they just don't have the money. Librans have impeccable taste, but they can't seem to translate it into reality like a Leo can.

What do you see them as? As charming companions who agree with your ideas, who appreciate your tastes, and who can live life on your level with no difficulty. When it comes to being decisive they are a waste of time, because they always see the other side to the argument as well, but you don't mind that. If they were at all decisive on their own, they might decide differently from you, and that would never do, would it? You see them as lazy, whereas they are simply ineffective, which is not the same thing. All in all, you like having them around. You value their opinions, but that doesn't mean you have to take their advice. They are decorative and companionable, and they don't get in the way when you're putting your foot down about something. Ideal, really.

If this relationship is limited to a light friendship, then the way to get the most value from it is to spend time doing the things where you can both contribute to the end result, such as some expensive, expansive, and artistic pursuit, where the Leo's generosity and the Libran's superlative taste can combine to produce something that could not have been achieved by either of you singly. Supper after the theatre sounds about right.

As lovers, the traditional romantic gestures will appeal to you both—the more stylish the better. You, Leo will have difficulty convincing the Libran that you are seriously in love; they take things very lightly, and steer clear of anything resembling commitment, even though the idea of marriage appeals to them a great deal. If you want to make it permanent you will have to be very patient, and not advertise your intention. Once married, you will have no problems other than making enough money to keep up with the style of life you both enjoy so much.

Leo-Scorpio

This is the partnership to go for if you like playing rough. Scorpios are hard fighters, and have the sort of determination which means that even when they lose they get even eventually. There is no way that you can conduct this relationship on a light and carefree level, even if you try to; it is strong and deep from the beginning. The rewards are high, and there is plenty of blazing passion on both sides: the downs are at least as deep as the ups are high, and the road is never smooth. If you fancy something you can get your teeth into, a relationship worth your time and strength, then try this one.

Scorpios do almost everything that you do in reverse. They don't put out energy as if it was free (which it is, to you, of course)—they collect it and store it within themselves. They like to be in control at all times, and this means that they have to know exactly what's going on, and what everybody is likely to do. Then they stay one jump ahead. Of course, it means that they have to do things their way, and that's where the opposition to you comes in. You know that you are only going to allow things to happen the way you say, because you like organizing things, and being at the centre, if not the front; Scorpios won't wear this at all. Your grand schemes are improperly thought out, in their view; there are possibilities which to you don't matter but to them seem important, and which must be catered for. What's more, it is obviously much better if they took over the whole affair so that you don't miss out anything else that's important. The arguments between you start at this point, and get worse.

You see them as unnecessarily interfering. Why can't they trust you to get things right? Everything works fine when you are left on your own—why do they have to try to control it? They see you as incredibly wasteful and dangerously open in all you do— how could you let everybody see what you are doing when they might want to use it against you? How could you be so generous with your time and money when it has to be so carefully guarded? They never see that you are open because you have nothing to hide, and generous because your energy comes for free; it never occurs to you that they might have something to hide, and that they might not have your facility for making things happen.

Yet you are linked to each other, in a way. The Scorpio's real goal is to be openly in power and publicly recognized for it, just as you are all the time; it is this which he admires in you above all else, and for which he forgives your excesses. You realize, of course, that your real power comes from within yourself, and you recognize the great store of that power inside the Scorpio, held down by his self-restrictive control; you would like to be able to share in, return to, and unite with, that power, and it is this which draws you to him, and for which you suffer his attempts to stifle your self-expression.

Any contact you make with a Scorpio turns into a power struggle after a very short time, so you cannot hope to have a mere amicable acquaintance. Either you will dislike each other quite fiercely, as the other elements in your horoscope add to the strain felt by your two Sun positions, or you will find yourselves exploring each other at deeper and deeper levels as the great energies you represent mingle and fuse with each other. A sexual relationship is the only one capable of handling the sort of current you two generate and this will become very powerful very quickly—real life-and-death stuff, playing with the energies of life itself. Arguments will be catastrophic, reconciliations sublimely uplifting; everything about it is more intense and on a bigger scale than a relationship with one of the other eleven signs. As a marriage, the same applies: you will fight for each other in public, and with each other in private. It won't be easy, but it won't be dull either.

Leo-Sagittarius

There is nobody on this earth you would rather waste your time with than a Sagittarian. The only person in the zodiac who makes you feel dull by comparison, and for whose place and talents you would gladly trade your own. Everything they do is a delight to you. They are lively, witty, and even more optimistic than you are; when you're together you feel you could take on the world. Fortunately for the rest of the world, you'll never get round to it because you're having too good a time imagining it all. Even if you went into business together you would need somebody to handle the actual mechanics of things, not to mention the finances. Between you, you are an ideas factory gone mad, with enough sheer ebullience to convince anybody of anything; but you're not too good on the practical side of things.

Sagittarius is confident and outgoing, as you are; but his confidence is the confidence of belief and of knowledge, whereas yours is the confidence of feeling only. Both of you are very forward-looking, far more interested in the immediate future than the past, and both absolutely sure that everything is going to turn out for the best. The difference in your attitudes is that you *feel* that things are going to be all right, and the Sagittarian *knows* that they are.

The Sagittarian seems to know everything there is to know about everything, and to share his knowledge freely. You recognize the generosity of spirit as being similar to your own, but you find the depth of his knowledge new and exciting: you sit there and soak it up eagerly. There isn't much in the world that you feel you would like more of, that you wish someone would give you, but whatever it is that Sagittarians put out is it.

You are also fascinated by their mobility. You know that you tend to stay in the same situation if it suits you, and you know, inside yourself, that this is because you don't think that you could be so successful if you had to adapt to changing surroundings the whole time. Sagittarians seem to be able to deal with things as they come up; they can move from one situation to another and still come out ahead. Is it all that knowledge, you ask yourself, that makes them so adaptable? No, it's Jupiter. Sagittarians are governed by a big planet, so they have big ideas, the same way you do, but Jupiter moves and the Sun doesn't. They use movement to stay at their best: a static Sagittarian is a sad person indeed.

They see you as a reminder that at the end of the day it isn't the material things that make life work, but the personal energies you can put in. They know that you always believe in yourself, and they find that an inspiring thought. Sometimes they wonder, with their changeable minds, whether being a giver rather than a taker is the right way to be—but five minutes in your company reminds them that to be self-confident, generous, and optimistic is the right way for them. You *refuel* Sagittarians, and that's what they like about you.

As friends, you will get on brilliantly, but don't expect to put any of your schemes into action! You are wonderfully restorative for each other's spirits.

As lovers, your relationship should be energetic and warm (two Fire signs). He will like to keep things moving and changeable, though, where you will be happy to stay with a good thing once you get one. Your dignity might get rumpled: Sagittarians have little time for ceremony, and when impulse overrides decorum they don't mind one bit—but you do! You could find yourself feeling a little old-fashioned as your lover teases your sentimental and romantic streak, but overall it is a stimulating affair, and one which you will enjoy.

As a marriage, you should have few problems. Even if you rule your household in typical Leonine manner, the Sagittarian won't complain, provided that you don't restrict his freedom. He needs to be able to move around and feel free: give him this and all will be well.

Leo-Capricorn

This one isn't easy. The partnership hinges on the essential difference between a person who is a success simply by existing, and a person who has made the attainment of success his life's work. On the surface and in public you can talk to each other as equals, but the approaches which led you both to the positions you occupy are very different.

Capricorn sees you as both the beginning and end of his own existence. You are successful, well liked, and have a reputation. People gather around you, listen to you, take notice of you. You are considered important. Quite often you are comfortably solvent, and when that isn't the case it doesn't seem to matter. Basically, you are a star. All that, the Capricorn wants. He wants to be seen as important, to be at the top of the pyramid. He sees you as being able to do what you do through applied self-confidence, which is quite perceptive of him, because that's more or less right. If he has confidence in himself and applies himself, he thinks, he will achieve the same result as you. As you were, he was; as you are, he will be, as the saying goes. What he doesn't see is that you have the Sun in you, radiating out through a person born when it was in its own sign. He doesn't have that. He has Saturn instead, which is cold and restrictive. when you apply yourself, you are applying warmth and sunlight to things, and who doesn't feel better when the Sun shines on them? When the Capricorn applies himself, he applies Saturn, which extinguishes warmth, adds weight, and gives a serious tone to things generally. Although the success will come in time, it will not come as easily as yours, nor can the Capricorn ever be you: the Sun does not shine out from him in the same way.

You see him differently. He gives shape to your achievements; by doing what he does without effort, you are seen as a success. A strange way of looking at things, I know, but public recognition and the acquisition of status symbols are in fact a Capricorn's definition of success, and you choose them as the means of communicating your importance to the rest of society. He works his way up the hierarchy of an organization, pointing out the shape of the hierarchy by his position; you place yourself at the top, in the ruling position, and know what it is that you are ruling because of him. Very wierd indeed.

It is very difficult for you to have any sort of a friendship. He is restrained and aloof, where you are open and generous. The Scorpio was restrained too, you may remember, but you could sense the power inside him, and that made him a challenge to you. The Capricorn isn't like that at all; inside him there is no raging passion. He is a genuinely quiet person; he has a strong sense of duty, a strong work ethic, and a low level of fun. There isn't a great deal to talk about between you.

If you are lovers, it is because the Capricorn sees you as a necessary step in his career. He is going to be cautious and rather reserved in his response to you, and you are going to be disappointed, because you would have liked some warmth and enthusiasm in return for your own, and you won't get any. A Capricorn won't move unless it is within a carefully defined framework; phrases like 'spontaneous initiative' are not part of his vocabulary. You might get to like his sense of humour as the affair develops, though, provided that you like your humour on the dry side.

As business partners you could do very well. The first thing to do is to forget your personal differences, and all about how you both got to be as good as you are; let him provide you with a framework for your creativity, and just watch your effectiveness increase. Provide him with the rewards he needs to see for his efforts in return, and you will never look back.

As a marriage, you would have to run things similarly to the business arrangement above; you would also have to provide the warmth and emotional input that a home and family require to be a success, because the cold Capricorn can't do it.

Leo-Aquarius

This partnership is a union of opposites in a zodiacal sense, since the two signs are exactly opposite to each other in the circle of the signs, but it is by no means a tense or argumentative relationship. Provided you stay in the public eye, and both spend time in the company of lots of other people, then you will have no problems.

To put it succinctly, Leo is concerned with an individual—himself—and Aquarius is concerned with the group, where individuality is lost in the crowd.

You are both outgoing people, who project their energies outwards from themselves rather than collect the energy that others put out, and this gets the relationship off to a good start; outgoing people find the active response of those similar to them encouraging, because it reminds them of themselves, which is good.

Aquarius is concerned with ideas and conversation, like Gemini and Libra were; like them he suffers from being rather less able to make things happen than you are, although he is the best of the Air signs in this respect. More than anything else he is an observer; he loves to be present at everything that is going on, loves the buzz of conversation and the excitement of social life, but would rather not be deeply involved. This is one of the major differences between you: you need to be at the centre of things, to be fully involved and the central source of energy for the whole situation, where he likes to be on the edge looking on, enjoying the show. Don't think he's timid—he isn't; he's just not got his heart in it the way you have. He is another Saturnine type, like the Capricorn; his interest is there, but it is cool—he doesn't radiate warmth the way you do.

He sees you as somebody who is much at home at a party or in company as he is, and as interested in life as he is, but whose personal involvement with everything is strange and mystifying. If I was as committed to my interests as that, he thinks, I could never turn my attention to anything new, and I would be unable to see what everybody else was doing. The whole point is to see what everybody else has to offer, and see how different people interact. The Leo needs to forget himself for a while.

It is a pity that so friendly a person can't really put himself into something one hundred per cent, you think. If he was as warm underneath as he is friendly on the top, and if he stopped drifting from one interest to another, he could be really likeable. The Aquarian needs to create something from his own efforts, by himself; then he'd see how good he can be.

You can't really understand each other, though you are made of much the same stuff. What you both enjoy immensely, though, is any kind of social function. You can become the heart of it, and the Aquarian can be the circulation, moving round from one person to another, keeping the flow of ideas and contact going, which he needs to do, as an Air sign. If the two of you have just each other's company for any length of time, you find him cold and withdrawn, and he finds you domineering; in a group both of you can shine, and enjoy each other to the full. This is the way to conduct the friendship if it is intended to stay as just that: in public, and in company.

Oddly enough, you both want to be different—but in different ways. You want to be the sort of person everybody wants to be, a sort of maximum intensity version of conventional virtues, but the Aquarian wants to be genuinely different, something else. In fact, he represents all the things which the members of a group don't have in common, where you are all the things they do. Funny, isn't it?

The juxtaposition of cool difference and warm conventionality becomes more marked if you are lovers, or are married. They work at a much lower emotional level than you, which makes them intriguing and aloof when they are lovers, but seemingly less caring as spouses. You will also find that their ideas on the content and management of a household are just as cool; your ideal of the welcoming hearth with a good table will take a bit of a bashing.

Leo-Pisces

This is a very special relationship. On the surface, it will look very bright and glossy, but you will know that it isn't like that underneath. On some levels, this relationship will exhaust you, and on others, it will give you the answers you have always been searching for. If you are quite happy with your active life, full of friends and things to do, then don't even bother with a Piscean acquaintance—but if you can't help feeling that it's all a bit empty, and that your soul needs nourishing as well as your body, then try this one. A Piscean is the Water into which the Leo Sun sinks at the end of its day, and from which it rises again. It's not the sort of relationship you can talk about over a quick half at lunchtime, though it *is* the sort you talk about by the end of the second bottle late in the evening. Nor are the alcoholic references merely decorations; Pisces has much to do with that substance and its effects.

Pisceans are either transparent, or chameleons; I'm not sure which. They can take on the attributes, and the life-style, of the person they are with at the time. When they are with you, they are Leonine, as Leonine as you are, and for that precise reason; you project yourself onto them, and they let you see exactly that. You are both creative, and you like that in each other. The difference is that you create your own world from the real world, and live in it; they create their own world from their imagination, and live in that *as if it were real*. Read the last sentence again—it's not easy. You are successful in the real world because you make it work for you, but they are in a different universe altogether. Life to you is simple and bold, like children's building bricks; life to them is all colours at once, impossibly complex and yet undefined, like the colours you see with your eyes shut.

You see Pisceans as frail and sensitive creatures, whose talent for playing roles to suit their surroundings amuses you; you see it as a parallel skill to your own ability to impose your personality on your surroundings. They seem to be from a different reality, and that interests you, because you would like to see what this other world is like.

They see you as hefty but essentially jolly individuals, whose genuine goodness of heart and optimism shows them how they can use the strength of their own personalities to make sense of the mass of impressions and emotions which seem to flood their minds. When life seems uncertain, you remind them of the goodness, the simplicity, and the fun of just being yourself.

Pisceans respond to everything; they find it difficult to focus on any one thing to the exclusion of everything else, and you can help them do this. At the same time, you will gain from having their heightened sensitivity at your disposal, especially if the two of you have some common interest that you can spend time on together. This is how your friendship actually works, and the more of this you do, the better you will appreciate each other.

As lovers, you will have an interesting time. Pisces will not have met your sheer creative power before, whereas it is the range and intensity of his emotional response that will surprise you. It is a union of the soul as well as the body—difficult to explain unless you've tried it and made it work.

Once you have formed a relationship that works on all levels, and there are a lot of them with a Pisces, you should have the basis of a lasting marriage. They offer you the long-term sastisfaction that you could never quite define, but knew you needed, and you offer them a reliable reference-point from which to build a life in the real world.

5. The Year within Each Day

You have probably wondered, in odd moments, why there are more than twelve varieties of people. You know more than twelve people who look completely different. You also know more than one person with the same Sun sign as yourself who doesn't look anything like you. You also know two people who look quite like each other, but who are not related, and do not have birthdays near each other, so can't be of the same Sun sign. You will have come to the conclusion that Sun signs and astrology don't work too well, because anyone can see that there are more than twelve sorts of people.

You will also have wondered, as you finished reading a newspaper or magazine horoscope, how those few sentences manage to apply to a twelfth of the nation, and why it is that they are sometimes very close to your true circumstances, and yet at other times miles off. You will have come to the conclusion that astrology isn't all that it might be, but some of it is, and that you like it enough to buy magazines for the horoscopes, and little books like this one.

It might be that there is some other astrological factor, or factors, which account for all the different faces that people have, the similarities between people of different Sun signs, and the apparent inconsistencies in magazine horoscopes. There are, indeed, lots of other astrological factors we could consider, but one in particular will answer most of the inconsistencies we have noticed so far.

It is the Ascendant, or rising sign. Once you know your Ascendant, you will see how you get your appearance, your way of working, your tastes, your preferences and dislikes, and your state of health (or not, as the case may be). It is perhaps of more use to you to consider yourself as belonging to your Ascendant sign, than your Sun sign. You have been reading the wrong newspaper horoscopes for years; you are not who you thought you were!

You are about to protest that you know when your birthday is. I'm sure you do. This system is not primarily linked to your birthday, though. It is a smaller cogwheel in the clockwork of the heavens, and we must come down one level from where we have been standing to see its movements. Since astrology is basically the large patterns of the sky made small in an individual, there are a number of 'step-down' processes where the celestial machinery adjusts itself to the smaller scale of mankind; this is one of them.

Here's the theory:

Your birthday pinpoints a particular time during the year. The Sun appears to move round the strip of sky known as the zodiac during the course of the year. In reality, of course, our planet, Earth, moves round the Sun once a year, but the great friendly feature of astrology is that it always looks at things from our point of view; so, we think we stand still, and the Sun appears to move through the zodiac. On a particular day of importance, such as your birthday, you can see which of the zodiac signs the Sun is in, pinpoint how far it has gone in its annual trip round the sky, and then say 'This day is important to me, because it is my birthday; therefore this part of the sky is important to me because the Sun is there on my special day. What are the qualities of that part of the Sun's journey through the zodiac, and what are they when related to me?' The answer is what you usually get in a horoscope book describing your Sun sign.

Fine. Now let's go down one level, and get some more detail. The Earth rotates on its own axis every day. This means that, from our point of view, we stand still and the sky goes round us once a day. Perhaps you hadn't thought of it before, but that's how the Sun appears to move up and across the sky from sunrise to sunset. It's actually us who are moving, but we see it the other way round. During any day, then, your birthday included, the whole of the sky goes past you at some time or another; but at a particular moment of importance, such as the time that you were born, you can see where the Sun is, see which way up the sky is, and say, 'This moment is important to me, because I was born at this time; therefore the layout of the sky has the same qualities as I do. What are the qualities of the sky at this time of day, and what are they when related to me?'

You can see how you are asking the same questions one level lower down. The problem is that you don't know which bit of the sky is significant. Which bit do you look at? All you can see? All that you can't (it's spherical from your point of view, and has no joins; half of it is below the horizon, remember)?

How about directly overhead? A very good try; the point in the zodiac you would arrive at is indeed significant, and is used a lot by astrologers, but there is another one which is more useful still. The eastern horizon is the point used most. Why? Because it fulfils more functions than any other point. It gives a starting point which is easily measurable, and is even visible (remember, all astrology started from observations made before mathematics or telescopes). It is also the contact point between the sky and the earth, from our point of view, and thus symbolizes the relationship between the sky and mankind on the earth. Finally, it links the smaller cycle of the day to the larger one of the year, because the Sun starts its journey on the eastern horizon each day as it rises; and, if we are concerned with a special moment, such as the time of your birth, then the start of the day, or the place that it started, at any rate, is analogous to the start of your life. Remember that you live the qualities of the moment you were born for all of your life; you are that moment made animate.

The point in the zodiac, then, which was crossing the eastern horizon at the time you were born, is called the Ascendant. If this happened to be somewhere in the middle of Gemini, then you have a Gemini Ascendant, or Gemini rising, whichever phrase you prefer. You will see that this has nothing to do with the time

STAR TIME (HOURS): 0 1 2 3 4 5 6 7 8 9 10 11 12 13 14 15 16 17 18 19 20 21 22 23 0

	Star Time signs (left → right)
GLASGOW	LEO · VIRGO · LIBRA · SCORPIO · SAGITTARIUS · CAPRICORN · AQUARIUS · PISCES · ARIES · TAURUS · GEMINI · CANCER · LEO
MANCHESTER	LEO · VIRGO · LIBRA · SCORPIO · SAGITTARIUS · CAPRICORN · AQUARIUS · PISCES · ARIES · TAURUS · GEMINI · CANCER
LONDON	LEO · VIRGO · LIBRA · SCORPIO · SAGITTARIUS · CAPRICORN · AQUARIUS · PISCES · ARIES · TAURUS · GEMINI · CANCER

CANCER

Different signs are on the horizon at different times according to where you live, as you can see. This is because of the difference in latitude. If you live in between the places given, you can make a guess from the values here. To compensate for longitude, subtract twelve minutes from your birthtime if you live in Glasgow, Liverpool or Cardiff; ten minutes for Edinburgh or Manchester, and six minutes for Leeds, Tyneside, or the West Midlands. *Add* four minutes for Norwich.

of year that you were born, only with the time of day.

Have a look at the diagrams on page 72, which should help explain things. If two people are born on the same day, but at different times, then the Ascendant will be different, and the Sun and all the other planets will be occupying different parts of the sky. It makes sense to assume, then, that they will be different in a number of ways. Their lives will be different, and they will look different. What they will have in common is the force of the Sun in the same sign, but it will show itself in different ways because of the difference in time and position in the sky.

How do you know which sign was rising over the eastern horizon when you were born? You will have to work it out. In the past, the calculation of the Ascendant has been the subject of much fuss and secrecy, which astrologers exploit to the full, claiming that only they can calculate such things. It does take some doing, it is true, but with a few short cuts and a calculator it need only take five minutes.

Here is the simplest routine ever devised for you to calculate your own Ascendant, provided that you know your time of birth. Pencil your answers alongside the stages as you go, so you know where you are.

1. Count forwards from 23 July to your birthday: 23 July is 1, 24 July is 2, and so on.
   Total days: .....*3*..

2. Add 304 to this. New total is: ....*30.7*...............

3. Divide by 365, and then

4. Multiply by 24. Answer is now: ...*20:0186301*......
   (Your answer by now is between 0 and 24. If it isn't, you have made a mistake somewhere. Go back and try again.)

5. Add your time of birth, in 24-hour clock time. If you were born at 3 p.m., that means 15. If you were born in Summer Time, take one hour off. If there are some spare minutes, your calculator would probably like them in decimals, so it's 0.1 of an hour for each six minutes. 5.36 p.m. is 17.6, for example. Try to be as close as you can. New total is: ...*40.151763*....

6. If your total exceeds 24, subtract 24. Your answer must now be between 0 and 24. Answer is: . . . .

7. You have now got the time of your birth not in clock time, but in sidereal, or star, time, which is what astrologers work in. Page 72 has a strip diagram with the signs of the zodiac arranged against a strip with the values 0 to 24, which are hours in star time. Look against the time you have just calculated, and you will see which sign was rising at the time you were born. For example, if your calculated answer is 10.456, then your Ascendant is somewhere in the middle of Scorpio.

What Does the Ascendant Do?

Broadly speaking, the Ascendant does two things. Firstly, it gives you a handle on the sky, so that you know which way up it was at the time you entered the game, so to speak; this has great significance later on in the book, when we look at the way you handle large areas of activity in your life such as your career, finances, and ambitions. Secondly, it describes your body. If you see your Sun sign as your mentality and way of thinking, then your Ascendant sign is your body and your way of doing things. Think of your Sun sign as the true you, but the Ascendant as the vehicle you have to drive through life. It is the only one you have, so you can only do with it the things of which it is capable, and there may be times when you would like to do things in a different way, but it 'just isn't you'. What happens over your life is that your Sun sign energies become specifically adapted to express themselves to their best via your Ascendant sign, and you become an amalgam of the two. If you didn't, you would soon become very ill. As a Leo with, say, a Libran Ascendant, you do things from a Leo motivation, but in a Libran way, using a Libran set of talents and abilities, and a Libran body. The next few sections of the book explain what this means for each of the Sun/Ascendant combinations.

Some note ought to be made of the correspondence between the Ascendant and the actual condition of the body. Since the

Ascendant sign represents your physical frame rather than the personality inside it, then the appearance and well-being of that frame is also determined by the Ascendant sign. In other words, if you have a Libra Ascendant, then you should look like a Libran, and you should be subject to illnesses in the parts of the body with a special affinity to that sign.

The Astrology of Illness

This is worth a book in itself, but it is quite important to say that the astrological view of illness is that the correlation between the individual and the larger universe is maintained. In other words, if you continue over a long period of time with a way of behaviour that denies the proper and necessary expression of your planetary energies, then the organ of your body which normally handles that kind of activity for your body systems will start to show the stresses to you. A simple example: Gemini looks after the lungs, which circulate air, and from which oxygen is taken all over the body. Gemini people need to circulate among a lot of people, talking and exchanging information. They act as the lungs of society, taking news and information everywhere. They need to do this to express their planetary energies, and society needs them to do this or it is not refreshed, and does not communicate. You need your lungs to do this, too. Lungs within people, Geminis within society: same job, different levels. If you keep a Gemini, or he keeps himself, through circumstance or ignorance, in a situation where he cannot talk or circulate, or where he feels that his normal status is denied, then he is likely to develop lung trouble. This need not be anything to do with a dusty atmosphere, or whether he smokes, although obviously neither of those will help; they are external irritants, and this is an internal problem caused by imbalance in the expression of the energies built into him since birth. In the sections which follow, all the observations on health are to do with how the body shows you that certain behaviour is unbalancing you and causing unnecessary stress; problems from these causes are alleviated by listening to yourself and changing your behaviour.

Your Ascendant

Aries Ascendant

If you have Aries rising, you are an uncommon individual, because Aries only rises for about fifty minutes out of the twenty-four hour day. You must have been born in the late evening or else you have got your sums wrong somewhere.

What you are trying to do with yourself is project a Leonine personality through an Arian vehicle. You will always be trying to do things faster than anybody else, and this can lead to hastiness and a certain degree of accident-proneness. What you see as the correct way to do things involves immediate action by the most direct method, to secure instant, and measurable, results. You feel that unless you are directly and personally responsible for doing things, then they cannot be done, not only because you believe that only you can do them properly, but because you get no satisfaction from letting anybody else do anything. Personal experience of everything is the only way you learn; reading about it, or watching it, does nothing for you.

You are likely to have headaches as a recurring problem if you push yourself too hard, and you should watch your blood pressure too. Mars, ruling Aries, is a strong and forceful planet, and it is bound to get you a little over-stressed at times. You are also likely to have problems digesting things properly. Astrologically, all illnesses apply to your external condition as well as your internal condition, so think carefully; when your head aches you are banging it too hard against a problem which cannot be overcome that way, and when you are not digesting properly, you have not understood the implications of what you have taken on. In both cases, allow time to think and consider.

Taurus Ascendant

You were born at around midnight if you have Taurus rising. Taureans are generally fond of food—do you celebrate your birth-time by sneaking down to the fridge for a midnight snack? You should have all the Taurean physical characteristics: quite thick-set, big around the neck and shoulders sometimes, and with large hands. You should have a broad mouth, and large eyes, which are very attractive. You should also have a good voice—not only as a singing voice, but one which is pleasant to listen to in conversation too.

The Taurean method for getting things done is to look forward to, and then enjoy, the material reward for one's efforts. It is part of Taurean thinking that if you can't touch it, buy it, own it or eat it, it isn't real and it isn't worth much. You will also be concerned to keep what is yours, not to waste your energies on what won't gain you anything or increase your possessions, and not to attempt anything which you don't think you have more than a chance of achieving.

Taureans do have taste; not only taste for food, which they love, but artistic taste, which they develop as a means of distinguishing things of value which they would then like to acquire and gain pleasure from owning. Unlike the Capricorn way of doing things, which values quality because it is valued by others, Taureans enjoy their possessions for themselves. The drawback to the Taurean approach is the lack of enterprise, and the unwillingness to try things just for the fun of it.

Taurean Ascendant people have throat and glandular problems, and all problems associated with being overweight. They can also have back and kidney problems caused as a result of an unwillingness to let things go in their external life. A lighter touch is needed in the approach to problems of possession; shedding unwanted or outworn things in a desirable process.

Gemini Ascendant

If you have a Gemini Ascendant you were born in the small hours of the morning. You should have expressive hands and a wide range of gestures which you use as you speak (ask your friends!) and you are perhaps a little taller than average, or than other members of your family. Gemini Ascendant people also have dark hair, if there is any possibility of it in their parents' colouring, and quick, penetrating eyes which flash with amusement and mischief; Gemini Ascendant women have very fine eyes indeed.

The Gemini approach to things, which you find yourself using, is one in which the idea of a thing is seen as being the most useful, and in which no time must be lost in telling it to other people so that they can contribute their own ideas and responses to the discussion. The performance of the deed is of no real importance in the Gemini view; somebody else can do that. Ideas and their development are what you like to spend time on, and finding more people to talk to, whose ideas can be matched to your own, seems to you to offer the most satisfaction.

There are two snags to the Gemini approach. The first is that there is a surface quality to it all, in which the rough outline suffices, but no time is spent in development or long-term experience. It may seem insignificant, but there is some value in seeing a project through to the end. The second snag is similar, but is concerned with time. The Gemini approach is immediate, in that it is concerned with the present or the near future. It is difficult for a Gemini Ascendant person to see farther than a few months into the future, if that; it is even more difficult for him to extend his view sideways in time to see the impact of his actions on a wider scene. Both of these things he will dismiss as unimportant.

Gemini Ascendant people suffer from chest and lung maladies, especially when they cannot communicate what they want to or need to, or when they cannot circulate socially in the way that they would like. They also have problems eliminating wastes from their bodies, through not realizing the importance of ending things as well as beginning them. In both cases, thinking and planning on a broader scale than usual, and examination of the past to help make better use of the future, is beneficial.

Cancer Ascendant

You were born before dawn if you have your Ascendant in Cancer and your Sun in Leo. The Cancerian frame, through which you project your energies, may mean that you appear rounder and less imposing than other Leos. Your energies are in no way diminished; in fact, you are likely to be even more expansive, and be described in newspaper clichés like 'small in stature, but big in every other respect'. Your face could be almost cherubic, and you could have small features in a pale complexion with grey eyes and brown hair. The key to the Cancer frame is that it is paler than usual, less well defined, and has no strong colouring. Strong noses and red hair do not come from a Cancerian Ascendant.

The Cancerian approach to things is highly personal. All general criticisms are taken personally, and all problems in any procedure for which they have responsibility are seen as personal failings. You will be concerned to use your energies for the safe and secure establishment of things from the foundations up, so that you know that whatever you have been involved in has been done properly, and is unlikely to let you down in any way; you are concerned for your own safety and reputation. The other side of this approach is that you can be a little too concerned to make sure everything is done personally, and be unwilling to entrust things to other people. Not only does this overwork you, it seems obsessive and uncooperative to others.

The Cancer Ascendant person has health problems with the maintenance of the flow of fluids in his body, and a tendency to stomach ulcers caused by worry. Cancer Ascendant women should pay special attention to their breasts, since the affinity between the sign, the Moon as ruler of all things feminine, and that particular body system means that major imbalances in the life are likely to show there first. There could also be some problems with the liver and the circulation of the legs; the answer is to think that, metaphorically, you do not have to support everybody you know: they can use their own legs to stand on, and you do not have to feed them either.

Leo Ascendant

You were born at dawn if you have Leo as an Ascendant sign as well as a Sun sign. Leo, as the determinant of the physical characteristics, makes itself known by the lion of the sign—you can always spot the deep chest, proud and slightly pompous way of walking, and, more often than not, the hair arranged in some sort of a mane, either full or taken back off the face, and golden if possible. Leo Ascendant people have strong voices and a definite presence to them. A Leo Ascendant will bring to the fore any hereditary tendency to golden colouring, so reddish or golden hair, or a rosy complexion may be in evidence, as will a heavy build in the upper half of the body.

The Leonine way of doing things is to put yourself in the centre and work from the centre outwards, making sure that everybody knows where the commands are coming from. It is quite a tiring way of working; you need to put a lot of energy into it, because you are acting as the driving force for everybody else. Preferred situations for this technique are those where you already know, more or less, what's going to happen; this way you are unlikely to be thrown off balance by unexpected developments. The grand gesture belongs to the Leo method; it works best if all processes are converted into theatrical scenes, with roles acted rather than lived. Over-reaction, over-dramatization, and over-indulgence are common, but the approach is in essence kind-hearted and well-meant. Children enjoy being with Leo Ascendant people, and they enjoy having children around them. The flaws in the approach are only that little gets done in difficult circumstances where applause and appreciation are scarce commodities, and that little is attempted that is really new and innovatory.

The health problems of the Leo Ascendant person come from the heart, and also from the joints, which suffer from mobility problems. These both come from a lifetime of being at the centre of things and working for everybody's good, and from being too stiff and unwilling to try any change in position. The remedy, of course, is to be more flexible, and to allow your friends to repay the favours they owe you.

Virgo Ascendant

A birth around breakfast time puts Virgo on the Ascendant. Physically, this should make you slim and rather long, especially in the body; even if you have broad shoulders you will still have a long waist. There is a neatness to the features, but nothing notable; hair is brown, but again nothing notable. The nose and chin are often well-defined, and the forehead is often both tall and broad; the voice can be a little shrill and lacks penetration.

The Virgoan Ascendant person does not have an approach to life; he has a *system*. He analyses everything and pays a lot of attention to the way in which he works. It is important to the person with Virgo rising not only to be effective, but to be efficient; you can always interest them in a new or better technique. They watch themselves work, as if from a distance, all the while wondering if they can do it better. They never mind repetition; in fact they quite enjoy it, because as they get more proficient they feel better about things. A Leo with a Virgo Ascendant will want to know how anything and everything works; you will not be able to take anything for granted, and will have to devote all your attention to things until you have mastered their intricacies for yourself. There is a willingness to help others, to be of service through being able to offer a superior technique, inherent in the Virgo way of doing things, which prevents Virgo rising people from being seen as cold and unfriendly. The problems in the Virgo attitude are a tendency to go into things in more detail than is necessary, and to be too much concerned with the 'proper' way to do things.

People with a Virgo Ascendant are susceptible to intestinal problems and circulatory problems, and may be prone to poor sight. All of these are ways in which the body registers the stresses of being too concerned with digesting the minutiae of things which are meant to be passed through anyway, and by not getting enough social contact. The remedy is to lift your head from your workbench sometimes, admit that the act is sometimes more important than the manner of its performance, and not to take things too seriously.

Libra Ascendant
You were born in the middle of the morning if have Libra rising; it will give you a pleasant and approachable manner which will do a great deal to hide your anxieties and prevent people thinking anything but the best of you. You should be tallish, and graceful, as all Libra Ascendant people tend to be, have a clear

complexion, and often blue eyes, set in an oval face with finely formed features.

The Libra Ascendant person has to go through life at a fairly relaxed pace. The sign that controls his body won't let him feel rushed or anxious; if that sort of thing looks likely, then he will slow down a little until the panic's over. There is a need to see yourself reflected in the eyes of others, and so you will form a large circle of friends. You define your own opinion of yourself through their responses to you, rather than being sure what you want, and not caring what they think.

The drawback to the Libran approach is that unless you have approval from others, you are unlikely to do anything on your own initiative, or at least you find it hard to decide on a course of action. You always want to do things in the way which will cause the least bother to anyone, and to produce an acceptable overall result; sometimes this isn't definite enough, and you need to know what you do want as well as what you don't.

The Libran Ascendant makes the body susceptible to all ailments of the kidneys and of the skin; there may also be trouble in the feet. The kidney ailments are from trying to take all the problems out of life as you go along. Sometimes it's better simply to attack a few of the obstacles and knock them flat in pure rage.

Scorpio Ascendant

You were probably born around noon if you have Scorpio for your Ascendant sign. This will make for great success in your chosen career, whatever it is. No matter what the job is, being born around the middle of the day guarantees public prominence whether you want it or not.

A Scorpio Ascendant should give you a dark and powerful look, with a solid build, though not necessarily over-muscled, Scorpio Ascendant people tend to have a very penetrating and level way of looking at others, which is often disconcerting. Any possible darkness in the colouring is usually displayed, with dark complexions and dark hair, often thick and curly, never fine.

The Scorpio Ascendant person usually does things in a controlled manner. He is not given to explosive releases of energy unless they are absolutely necessary; even then, not often. He knows, or feels (a better word, since the Scorpionic mind makes decisions as a result of knowledge gained by feeling rather than thinking), that he has plenty of energy to spare, but uses it in small and effective doses, each one suited to the requirements of the task at hand. It does not seem useful to him to put in more effort than is strictly necessary for any one activity; that extra energy could be used somewhere else. The idea that overdoing things for their own sake is sometimes fun because of the sheer exhilaration of the release of energy does not strike a responsive chord in the Scorpio body, nor even much understanding and perception of a situation which exists at more than one level. If anything is complicated, involving many activities and many people, with much interaction and many side issues which must be considered, then the Scorpio ascendant person sees it all and understands all of it in its minutest detail. They feel, and understand, the responses from all of their surroundings at once, but do not necessarily feel involved with them unless they choose to make a move. When they do move, they will have the intention of transforming things, making them different to conform to their ideas of how things need to be arranged.

Scorpio Ascendant people are unable simply to possess and look after anything; they must change it and direct it their way, activity; that extra energy could be used somewhere else. The idea that overdoing things for their own sakes is sometimes fun because of the sheer exhilaration of the release of energy does not strike a responsive chord in the Scorpio body, nor even much understanding. There is, however, understanding and perception of a situation which exists at more than one level. If anything is complicated, involving many activities and many people, with much interaction and many side issues which must be considered, then the Scorpio Ascendant person sees it all and understands all of it, in its minutest detail. They feel, and understand, the responses from all of their surroundings at once, but do not necessarily feel involved with them unless they choose to make a move. When they do move, they will have the intention of transforming things, making them different to conform to their ideas of how things need to be arranged.

Scorpio Ascendant people are unable simply to possess and look after anything; they must change it and direct it their way, and this can be a disadvantage.

Scorpio illnesses are usually to do with the genital and excretory systems; problems here relate to a lifestyle in which things are thrown away when used, or sometimes rejected when there is still use in them. It may be that there is too much stress on being the founder of the new, and on organizing others; this will bring head pains, and illnesses of that order. The solution is to take on the existing situation as it is, and look after it without changing any of it.

Sagittarius Ascendant

It would have been mid-afternoon when you were born for you to have a Sagittarius Ascendant. If you have, you should be taller than average, with a sort of sporty, leggy look to you; you should have a long face with pronounced temples (you may be balding there if you are male), a well-coloured complexion, clear eyes, and brown hair. A Grecian nose is sometimes a feature of this physique.

The Sagittarian Ascendant gives a way of working that is based on mobility and change. This particular frame can't keep still and is much more comfortable walking than standing, more comfortable lounging or leaning than sitting formally. You tend to be in a bit of a hurry; travelling takes up a lot of your time, because you enjoy it so. It is probably true to say that you enjoy the process of driving more than whatever it is that you have to do when you get there. You probably think a lot of your car, and you are likely to have one which is more than just a machine for transport—you see it as an extension, a representation even, of yourself. People will notice how outgoing and friendly you seem to be, but they will need to know you for some time before they realize that you enjoy meeting people more than almost anything else, and you dislike being with the same companions all the time. There is a constant restlessness in you; you will feel that being static is somehow unnatural, and it worries you. You are an optimist, but can also be an opportunist, in that you see no reason to stay doing one thing for a moment longer than it interests you. The inability to stay and develop a situation or give long-term commitment to anything is the biggest failing of this sign's influence.

A person with Sagittarius rising can expect to have problems with his hips and thighs, and possibly in his arterial system; this is to do with trying to leap too far at once, in all senses. You may also have liver and digestive problems, again caused by haste on a long-term scale. The remedy is to shorten your horizons and concentrate on things nearer home.

Capricorn Ascendant

It must have been late afternoon when you were born for you to have a Capricorn Ascendant. This sign often gives a small frame, quite compact and built to last a long time, the sort that doesn't need a lot of feeding and isn't big enough or heavy enough to break when it falls over. The face can be narrow and the features small; often the mouth points downwards at the corners, and this doesn't change even when the person smiles or laughs.

The Capricorn sees life as an ordered, dutiful struggle. There is a great deal of emphasis placed on projecting and maintaining appearances, both in the professional and the personal life; the idea of 'good reputation' is one which everybody with Capricorn rising, whatever their sun sign, recognizes at once. There is a sense of duty and commitment which the Sagittarian Ascendant simply cannot understand; here the feeling is that there are things which need doing, so you just have to set to and get them done. Capricorn Ascendant people see far forwards in time, anticipating their responsibilities for years to come, even if their Sun sign does not normally function this way; in such cases they apply themselves to one problem at a time, but can envisage a succession of such problems, one after another, going on for years.

The disadvantages of this outlook are to do with its static nature. There is often a sense of caution that borders on the paranoid, and while this is often well disguised in affluent middle-class middle age, it seems a little odd in the young. This tends to make for a critical assessment of all aspects of a new venture before embarking on it, and as a result a lot of the original impetus is lost. This makes the result less than was originally hoped in many cases, and so a cycle of disappointment and unadventurousness sets in, which is difficult to break. The Capricorn Ascendant person is often humourless, and can seem determined to remain so.

These people have trouble in their joints, and break bones from time to time, entirely as a result of being inflexible. On a small scale this can be from landing badly in an accident because the Capricorn Ascendant keeps up appearances to the very end, refusing to believe that an accident could be happening to him: on a large scale, a refusal to move with the times can lead to the collapse of an outmoded set of values when they are swept away by progress, and this breaking up of an old structure can also cripple. They can get lung troubles, too, as a result of not taking enough fresh air, or fresh ideas. The best treatment is to look after their families rather than their reputation, and to think about the difference between stability and stagnation.

Aquarius Ascendant

Having an Aquarius Ascendant means that you were born around sunset. This will make you chattier than you would otherwise have been, with a strong interest in verbal communication. There is a certain clarity, not to say transparency, about the Aquarian physique. It is usually tall, fair, and well shaped, almost never small or dark. There is nothing about the face which is particularly distinctive; no noticeable colouring, shape of nose, brows, or any other feature. It is an average sort of face, cleanly formed and clear.

The person with an Aquarian Ascendant wants to be independent. Not violently so, not the sort of independence that fights its way out of wherever it feels it's been put, just different from everybody else. Aquarius gives your body the ability to do things in ways perhaps not done before; you can discover new techniques and practices for yourself, and don't need to stay in the ways you were taught. There is a willingness to branch out, to try new things; not a Scorpionic wish to make things happen the way you want, but an amused curiosity which would just like to see if things are any better done a different way. There is no need for you to convince the world that your way is best: it only needs to suit you.

Of course, an Aquarian needs to measure his difference against others, and therefore you feel better when you have a few friends around you to bounce ideas off, as well as showing them how you're doing things in a slightly different way. You function best in groups, and feel physically at ease when you're not the only person in the room. You are not necessarily the leader of the group; just a group member. Group leaders put their energy into the group, and you draw strength and support from it, so you are unlikely to be the leader, though paradoxically all groups work better for having you in them.

A handicap arising from an Aquarian Ascendant is that you are unlikely to really feel passionately involved with anything, and this may mean that unless you have support from your friends and colleagues you will be unable to muster the determination necessary to overcome really sizeable obstacles in your chosen career.

You are likely to suffer from diseases of the circulation and in your lower legs and ankles; these may reflect a life where too much time is spent trying to be independent, and not enough support is sought from others. You may also get stomach disorders and colds because you are not generating enough heat: get more involved in things and angrier about them!

Pisces Ascendant
You were born late in the evening if you have Pisces rising. Like Aries rising, Pisces is only possible as an Ascendant for about fifty minutes, so there aren't many of you around. Pisces Ascendant people are on the small side, with a tendency to be a

bit pale and fleshy. They are not very well coordinated and so walk rather clumsily, despite the fact that their feet are often large. They have large, expressive, but rather sleepy-looking eyes.

As a Leo with Pisces rising, you will prefer to let things come to you than go out and look for them. You will have a very secure and private home, which functions as both a retreat and an escape for you. Although you enjoy being presented with a variety of possible actions, you feel that all of them are a little risky, and you would really prefer to stay as you are. The slightest thought of doing anything decisive or assertive has you looking around for an escape route at once. Only when backed into a corner will you make a positive move, and that is merely to get you out of the corner so that you can return to a state of indecisiveness again. You are very protective of yourself, more so than the other Leos; they will trust to luck, but you want to be sure beforehand that you are not going to be trapped in a situation you would rather not be in.

The major problem with a Pisces Ascendant is this inability to be active rather than reactive; you would rather be reacting to outside influences than generating your own movements from within yourself.

A Piscean Ascendant gives problems with the feet and the lymphatic system; this has connections with the way you move in response to external pressures, and how you deal with things which invade your system from outside. You may also suffer from faint-heartedness—literally as well as metaphorically. The remedy is to be more definite and less influenced by opinions other than your own.

6. Three Crosses: Areas of Life that Affect Each Other

If you have already determined your Ascendant sign from page 73, and you have read 'The Meaning of the Zodiac' on page 11, you can apply that knowledge to every area of your life with revealing results. Instead of just looking at yourself, you can see how things like your career and your finances work from the unique point of view of your birth moment.

You will remember how the Ascendant defined which way up the sky was. Once you have it the right way up, then you can divide it into sectors for different areas of life, and see which zodiac signs occupy them. After that, you can interpret each sector of sky in the light of what you know about the zodiac sign which fell in it at the time that you were born.

Below there is a circular diagram of the sky, with the horizon splitting it across the middle. This is the way real horoscopes are usually drawn. In the outer circle, in the space indicated, write the name of your Ascendant sign, not your Sun sign (unless they are the same, of course. If you don't know your time of birth, and so can't work out an Ascendant, use your Sun sign). Make it overlap sectors 12 and 1, so that the degree of your Ascendant within that sign is on the eastern horizon. Now fill in the rest of the zodiac around the circle in sequence, one across each sector boundary. If you've forgotten the sequence, look at the diagram on page 16. When you've done that, draw a symbol for the Sun (☉—a circle with a point at its centre) in one of the sectors which has your Sun sign at its edge. Think about how far through the sign your Sun is; make sure that you have put it in the right sector. Whichever sector this is will be very important to you;

having the Sun there gives a bias to the whole chart, like the weight on one side of a locomotive wheel. You will feel that the activities of that sector (or house, as they are usually called) are most in keeping with your character, and you feel comfortable doing that sort of thing.

Make sure you have got your sums right. As a Leo born in the early evening, you might well have Capricorn rising, and the Sun in the eighth house, for example.

Now is the time to examine the twelve numbered sections of your own sky, and see what there is to be found.

Angular Houses: 1, 4, 7, 10

These are the houses closest to the horizon and the vertical, reading round in zodiacal sequence. The first house is concerned with you yourself as a physical entity, your appearance, and your health. Most of this has been dealt with in the section on

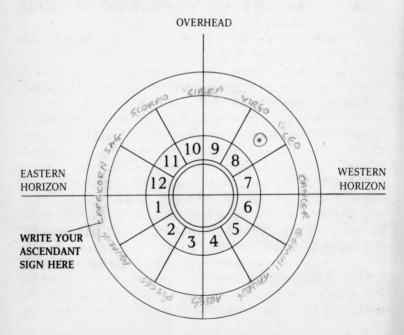

Ascendants. If you have the Sun here, it simply doubles the impact of your Sun sign energies.

Opposite to you is the seventh house, which concerns itself with everybody who is not you. Partners in a business sense, husbands, wives, enemies you are actually aware of (and who therefore stand opposed to you in plain sight) and any other unclassified strangers all belong in the seventh house. You see their motivation as being of the opposite sign to your Ascendant sign, as being something you are not. If you have Capricorn rising, you see them as behaving, and needing to be treated, which is perhaps more accurate, in a Cancerian manner. This is how you approach seventh-house things. Use the keywords from 'The Meaning of the Zodiac' (p. 17) to remind yourself what this is. If you have the Sun in the seventh house you are your own best partner: you may marry late in life, or not at all. Perhaps your marriage will be unsuccessful. It is not a failure; it is simply that you are to a very great extent self-supporting, and have neither the ability nor the need to share yourself completely with another.

The whole business of the first and the seventh is to do with 'me and not-me'. For the personal energies of this relationship to be shown in tangible form, it is necessary to look at the pair of houses whose axis most squarely crosses the first/seventh axis. This is the fourth/tenth. The tenth is your received status in the world, and is the actual answer to the question 'What do you take me for?' No matter what you do, the world will find it best to see you as doing the sort of thing shown by the sign in the tenth house. Eventually, you will start to pursue that kind of activity anyway, because in doing so you get more appreciation and reward from the rest of society.

Your efforts in dealing with others, which is a first/seventh thing, have their result in the tenth, and their origins in the fourth. Expect to find clues there to your family, your home, the beliefs you hold most dear, and the eventual conclusion to your life (not your death, which is a different matter). If you have the Sun in the tenth, you will achieve some measure of prominence or fame; if your Sun is in the fourth, you will do well in property, and your family will be of greater importance to you than is usual.

There is, of course, some give and take between the paired houses. Giving more time to yourself in the first house means that you are denying attention to the seventh, your partner; the reverse also applies. Giving a lot of attention to your career, in the tenth house, stops you from spending quite so much time as you might like with your family or at home. Spending too much time at home means that you are out of the public eye. There is only so much time in a day; what you give to one must be denied to the other.

This cross of four houses defines most people's lives: self, partner, home, and career. An over-emphasis on any of these is to the detriment of the other three, and all the arms of the cross feel and react to any event affecting any single member.

If these four houses have cardinal signs on them in your chart, then you are very much the sort of person who feels that he is in control of his own life, and that it is his duty to shape it into something new, personal, and original. You feel that by making decisive moves with your own circumstances you can actually change the way your life unfolds, and enjoy steering it the way you want it to go.

If these four houses have fixed signs on them in your chart, then you are the sort of person who sees the essential shape of your life as being one of looking after what you were given, continuing in the tradition, and ending up with a profit at the end of it all. Like a farmer, you see yourself as a tenant of the land you inherited, with a responsibility to hand it on in at least as good a condition as it was when you took it over. You are likely to see the main goal in all life's ups and downs as the maintenance of stability and enrichment of what you possess.

If these four houses have mutable signs on them in your chart, then you are much more willing to change yourself to suit circumstances than the other two. Rather than seeing yourself as the captain of your ship, or the trustee of the family firm, you see yourself as free to adapt to challenges as they arise, and if necessary to make fundamental changes in your life, home and career to suit the needs of the moment. You are the sort to welcome change and novelty, and you don't expect to have anything to show for it at the end of the day except experience. There is a strong sense of service in the mutable signs, and if you spend your life working for the welfare of others, then they will have something to show for it while you will not. Not in physical terms, anyway; you will have had your reward by seeing your own energies transformed into their success.

The Succedent Houses: 2, 5, 8, 11

These houses are called succedent because they succeed, or follow on from, the previous four. Where the angular houses define the framework of the life, the succedent ones give substance, and help develop it to its fullest and richest extent, in exactly the same way as fixed signs show the development and maintenance of the elemental energies defined by the cardinal signs.

The second house and the eighth define your resources; how much you have to play with, so to speak. The fifth and eleventh show what you do with it, and how much you achieve. Your immediate environment is the business of the second house. Your tastes in furniture and clothes are here (all part of your immediate environment, if you think about it) as well as your immediate resources, food and cash. Food is a resource because without it you are short of energy, and cash is a resource for obvious reasons. If you have the Sun here you are likely to be fond of spending money, and fond of eating too! You are likely to place value on things that you can buy or possess, and judge your success by your bank balance.

Opposed to it, and therefore dealing with the opposite viewpoint, is the eighth house, where you will find stored money. Savings, bank accounts, mortgages, and all kinds of non-immediate money come under this house. So do major and irreversible changes in your life, because they are the larger environment rather than the immediate one. Surgical operations and death are both in the eighth, because you are not the same person afterwards, and that is an irreversible change. If you have the Sun in the eighth you are likely to be very careful with yourself, and not the sort to expose yourself to any risk; you are also not likely to be short of a few thousand when life gets tight, because eighth house people always have some extra resource tucked away somewhere. You are also likely to benefit from legacies, which are another form of long-term wealth.

To turn all this money into some form of visible wealth you must obviously do something with it, and all forms of self-expression and ambition are found in the fifth and the eleventh houses. The fifth is where you have fun, basically; all that you like to do, all that amuses you, all your hobbies are found there, and a look at the zodiac sign falling in that house in your chart will show you what it is that you like so much. Your children are a fifth-house phenomenon, too; they are an expression of yourself made physical, made from the substance of your body and existence, and given their own. If you have the Sun in the fifth house you are likely to be of a generally happy disposition, confident that life is there to be enjoyed, and sure that something good will turn up.

The eleventh house, in contrast, is not so much what you like doing as what you would like to be doing: it deals with hopes, wishes, and ambitions. It also deals with friends and all social gatherings, because in a similar manner to the first/seventh axis, anybody who is 'not-you' and enjoying themselves must be opposed to you enjoying yourself in the fifth house. If you have the Sun in the eleventh house, you are at your best in a group. You would do well in large organizations, possibly political ones, and will find that you can organize well. You have well-defined ambitions, and know how to realize them, using other people as supporters of your cause.

The oppositions in this cross work just as effectively as the previous set did: cash is either used or stored, and to convert it from one to the other diminishes the first. Similarly, time spent enjoying yourself does nothing for your ambitions and aims, nor does it help you maintain relationships with all the groups of people you know; there again, all work and no play . . .

If you have cardinal signs on these four houses in your chart, then you think that using all the resources available to you at any one time is important. Although what you do isn't necessarily important, or even stable, you want to have something to show for it, and enjoying yourself as you go along is important to you. To you, money is for spending, and how your friends see you is possibly more important to you than how you see yourself.

Fixed signs on these four houses will make you reticent, and careful of how you express yourself. You are possibly too busy with the important things of life as you see them, such as your career and long-term prospects, to give much attention to the way you live. You feel it is important to have things of quality, because you have a long-term view of life, and you feel secure when you have some money in the bank, but you don't enjoy your possessions and friends for your own sake. You have them because you feel that you should, not because they are reason enough in themselves.

Mutable signs on these four houses show a flexible attitude to the use of a resource, possibly because the angular houses show that you already have plenty of it, and it is your duty to use it well. You don't mind spending time and money on projects which to you are necessary, and which will have a measurable end result. You see that you need to spend time and effort to bring projects into a completed reality, and you are willing to do that as long as the final product is yours and worth having. You are likely to change your style of living quite frequently during your life, and there may be ambitions which, when fulfilled, fade from your life completely.

The Cadent Houses: 3, 6, 9, 12

The final four houses are called cadent either because they fall away from the angles (horizon and vertical axes), or because they fall towards them, giving their energy towards the formation of the next phase in their existence. Either way, affairs in these houses are nothing like as firm and active as those in the other two sets of four. It may be useful to think of them as being given to mental rather than physical or material activities.

The third and ninth houses are given to thought and speech, with the ninth specializing in incoming thoughts, such as reading, learning and belief (religions of all kinds are ninth-house things), while the third limits itself to speaking and writing, daily chat, and the sort of conversations you have every day. If you have the Sun in the third house, you will be a chatterbox. Talking is something you could do all day, and you love reading. Anything will do—papers, magazines, novels; as long as it has words in it you will like it. You will have the sort of mind that loves accumulating trivia, but you may find that serious study or hard learning is something that you cannot do.

The third house concerns itself with daily conversation, but the ninth is more withdrawn. Study is easy for a ninth-house person, but since all ideal and theoretical thought belongs here, the down-to-earth street-corner reality of the third house doesn't, and so the higher knowledge of the ninth finds no application in daily life. The third-ninth axis is the difference between practical street experience and the refined learning of a university. To give time to one must mean taking time from the other. If you have the Sun in the ninth, you are likely to have a very sure grasp of the theory of things, and could well be an instigator or director of large projects; but you are unable to actually do the things yourself. Knowledge is yours, but application is not.

How this knowledge gets applied in the production of something new is a matter of technique, and technique is the business of the sixth house. The way things get done, both for yourself and for other people's benefit, is all in the sixth. Everything you do on someone else's behalf is there, too. If you have the Sun in the sixth house, you are careful and considerate by nature, much concerned to make the best use of things and to do things in the best way possible. Pride of work and craftsmanship are guiding words to you; any kind of sloppiness is upsetting. You look after yourself, too; health is a sixth-house thing, and the Sun in the sixth sometimes makes you something of a hypochondriac.

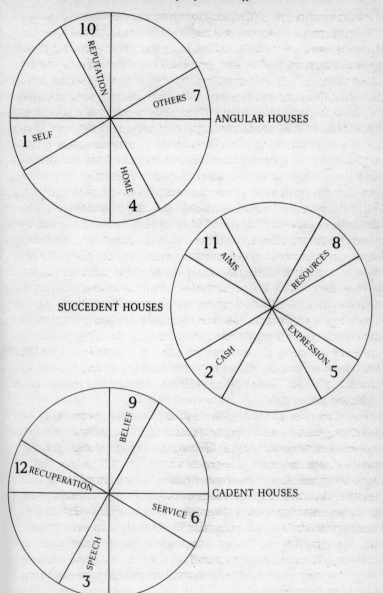

ANGULAR HOUSES

SUCCEDENT HOUSES

CADENT HOUSES

Opposed to the sixth, and therefore opposed to the ideas of doing things for others, mastering the proper technique, and looking after your physical health, is the twelfth house. This is concerned with withdrawing yourself from the world, being on your own, having time to think. Energy is applied to the job in hand in the sixth house, and here it is allowed to grow again without being applied to anything. Recuperation is a good word to remember. All forms of rest are twelfth-house concepts. If you have the Sun in the twelfth house you are an essentially private individual, and there will be times when you need to be on your own to think about things and recover your strength and balance. You will keep your opinions to yourself, and share very little of your emotional troubles with anyone. Yours is most definitely not a life lived out in the open.

These houses live in the shadow of the houses which follow them. Each of them is a preparation for the next phase. If your Sun is in any of these houses, your life is much more one of giving away than of accumulation. You already have the experience and the knowledge, and you will be trying to hand it on before you go, so to speak. Acquisition is something you will never manage on a permanent basis.

If these houses have Cardinal signs on them in your chart, then preparation for things to come is important to you, and you think in straight lines towards a recognized goal. You will have firm and rather simplistic views and beliefs about matters which are not usually described in such terms, such as morality and politics, and you will be used to saying things simply and with meaning. Deception and half-truths, even mild exaggeration, confuse you, because you do not think in that sort of way.

If fixed signs occupy these houses in your horoscope, your thinking is conservative, and your mind, though rich and varied in its imagination, is not truly original. You like to collect ideas from elsewhere and tell yourself that they are your own. You rely on changing circumstances to bring you variety, and your own beliefs and opinions stay fixed to anchor you in a changing world; unfortunately, this can mean a refusal to take in new ideas, shown in your behaviour as a rather appealing old-fashionedness.

Having mutable signs on these houses in your horoscope shows a flexible imagination, though often not a very practical one. Speech and ideas flow freely from you, and you are quick to adapt your ideas to suit the occasion, performing complete changes of viewpoint without effort if required. You seem. to have grasped the instinctive truth that mental images and words are not real, and can be changed or erased at will; you are far less inhibited in their use than the other two groups, who regard words as something at least as heavy as cement, and nearly as difficult to dissolve. Periods in the public eye and periods of isolation are of equal value to you; you can use them each for their best purpose, and have no dislike of either. This great flexibility of mind does mean, though, that you lack seriousness of approach at times, and have a happy-go-lucky view of the future, and of things spiritual, which may lead to eventual disappointments and regrets.

Houses are important in a horoscope. The twelve sectors of the sky correspond to the twelve signs of the zodiac, the difference being that the zodiac is a product of the Sun's annual revolution, and the houses are a product (via the Ascendant) of the Earth's daily revolution. They bring the symbolism down one level from the sky to the individual, and they answer the questions which arise when people of the same Sun sign have different lives and different preferences. The house in which the Sun falls, and the qualities of the signs in the houses, show each person's approach to those areas of his life, and the one which will be the most important to him.

Part 4

Leo Trivia

7. Tastes and Preferences

Clothes

It doesn't really matter what sort of clothes a Leo wears; the important thing, and the noticeable one, is the way he wears them. Leos have the uncanny ability to look good in anything at all—this is because they are expressing their own warmth, creativity, and confidence through the clothes they happen to have on at the time, and anything, worn well, looks good.

Given some sort of a choice, the Leo tries to wear things that suit him, and takes care to show off his physique. The Leo physique includes a prominent chest (it's where the heart, the Leo organ, lives) which always gives them a powerful and well-built look, especially given that they walk very upright and hold their heads high.

A few years ago, male Leos could be found literally showing their chests, usually with a gold medallion to draw attention to it. That fashion has now passed, but the taste for self-decoration is still there in every Leo, waiting for a chance to show itself. Recently the TV series 'Dynasty' has provided female Leos with an example of the style of their sign: the enlarged shoulders, making the upper half of the body more prominent, and the open display of wealth and decoration, are very Leonine indeed.

Male Leos are usually conservative in their dress sense, waiting until a style has become well established in public taste before adopting it for themselves. When they buy clothes, they always buy the most expensive available, and make sure it fits well; the idea is firstly to express the Leo's idea of his own quality, and secondly to provoke the admiration he so enjoys. His favourite colours are actually those of the Sun, such as gold, but it is outside conservative taste at the moment for men to dress in yellow and gold, so the Leo compromises with rich and royal colours instead, like maroon and deep blue. The love of gold is transferred to his jewellery. It is most unusual for a mature Leo male not to have at least a gold watch and a gold ring, and he often has much more.

Female Leos work along the same lines. They like their clothes to be flamboyant and obviously wealthy—and they show this by using real materials rather than synthetics whenever they can, including fur, of which they are very fond.

Food and Furnishings

Leos make wonderful hosts, and sometimes less than wonderful guests if you are trying to feed one. If they are giving the party, they are eager to show you that their parties are bigger, better, and more lavish than anything else you have ever seen, so you just go along and enjoy it. If they are a guest at a party, they have a tendency to tell everybody what they would have done if it were their party, which can be difficult.

Leos like eating large amounts of luxury foods; it is a way of showing their taste for the best in life, and their determination to enjoy it. Of course, a diet consisting entirely of rich delicacies brings its own problems, but that is another story. If you are trying to feed a Leo, a large and impressive piece of meat is the obvious choice, as is anything which contains oranges or lemons as a decoration or flavouring. This is because citrus fruits are solar fruit in astrological thought, and so will appeal to the solar sign, Leo.

Leos like their drinks to be big in flavour, so strong red wines are favourites. They also like to show exclusivity and opulence, so champagne is popular too. Even the beer has to be a luxury brew—Leos don't drink 'ordinary' beers. Unlike Taureans, who have a similar liking for good food, Leos don't like things too sweet.

A Leo's home is a luxurious place. Everything about it is there to remind both its owner and his guests that the owner is a very special individual. All the furnishings and fabrics will be on a grand scale, and very rich and heavy materials will have been used. In small rooms this can have an overpowering effect, and there is more than a slight possibility that the decoration will have been taken to the ridiculous. Leos are the sort of people whose taste runs to tiger-skin bathmats and gold-plated ashtrays.

The colours will be warm, and the central heating will have been turned up to match; solar people like solar warmth, and Leos are irritable and withdrawn when they feel cold. Naturally they will ensure that this doesn't happen to them in their own house.

Leos want their guests to feel comfortable, and to be impressed; there will be one or two large pictures on the walls, generally of a big subject grandly treated. Overall, the place is a palace; it is both a demonstration and a reminder of the standard of living a Leo expects.

Hobbies

Leonine hobbies are no mere pastimes or things dabbled in; if a Leo takes something up, he does it well enough to pursue it professionally. Leonine photographers do not take holiday snaps, they compose landscapes, they do their own processing and enlarging, and they exhibit the results. Leo sportsmen are professional sportsmen; the emphasis is on the individual disciplines, because Leos don't really fit into teams very well.

The great Leo interest is the theatre; it is the perfect vehicle for Leonine energy, since it enables you to express yourself to an audience, to be up in a place of prominence with the spotlight on you. There are, and have always been, many great Leo actors.

Leos are essentially creators; they paint, they make things in wood and metal—especially gold, their own planetary metal, if they can afford it—but it is the act of creation which is the important thing.

8. Leo Luck

Being lucky isn't a matter of pure luck. It can be engineered. What happens when you are lucky is that a number of correspondences are made between circumstances, people, and even material items, which eventually enable planetary energies to flow quickly and effectively to act with full force in a particular way. If you are part of that chain, or your intentions lie in the same direction as the planetary flow, then you say that things are going your way, or that you are lucky. All you have to do to maximize this tendency is to make sure you are aligned to the flow of energies from the planets whenever you want things to work your way.

It is regular astrological practice to try to reinforce your own position in these things, by attracting energies which are already strongly represented in you. For a Gemini, this means Mercury, of course, and therefore any 'lucky' number, colour, or whatever for a Leo is is simply going to be one of those which correspond symbolically with the attributes of the Sun.

The Sun's colours are yellow and gold; therefore a Leo person's lucky colours are yellow and gold, because by wearing it or aligning himself to it, for example by betting on a horse whose jockey's silks are yellow or gold, or supporting a sporting team whose colours include gold, he aligns himself to the energies of the Sun, and thereby recharges the solar energies that are already in him.

A Leo's preferred gemstone is a diamond, because of its brilliance and the reasons given above. Gemstones are seen as being able to concentrate or focus magical energies, and the colour of the stone shows its propensity to the energies of a particular planet. Other gemstones are sometimes quoted for Leo, such as the chrysolite or some rubies, but in most cases the colour is the key.

Because Leo is the fifth sign, your lucky number is 5; all combinations of numbers which add up to 5 by reduction work the same way, so you have a range to choose from. Reducing a number is done by adding its digits until you can go no further. As an example, take 698, $6 + 9 + 8 = 23$, and then $2 + 3 = 5$. There you are—698 is a lucky number for you, so to buy a car with those digits in its registration plate would make it a car which, while you had it, you were very fond of, and which served you well.

The Sun has its own number, which is 6. The same rules apply as they did with 5. The Sun also has its own day, Sunday (Sun Day), and Leo has a direction with which it is associated, the East. If you have something important to do, and you manage to put it into action on Sunday 6 May (month number 5, remember), then you will have made sure that you will get the result best suited to you, by aligning yourself to your own planet and helping its energies flow through you and your activity unimpeded.

The Sun also has a metal associated with it, and in the Middle Ages people wore jewellery made of their planetary metals for luck, or self-alignment and emphasis, whichever way you want to describe it. In the case of Leo and the Sun, that metal is gold. You are lucky—some of the planetary metals don't look very attractive made up into jewellery, but there is an almost unlimited range of beautiful items in gold for you to choose from.

There are plants and herbs for each planet, and foods too. Among the more edible plants are oranges and lemons, ginger, and saffron. Musk, the perfume ingredient, is solar, too, apparently.

There is almost no end to the list of correspondences between the planets and everyday items, and many more can be made if you have a good imagination. They are lucky for Leos if you know what makes them so, and if you believe them to be so; the essence of the process lies in linking yourself and the object of your intent with some identifiable token of your own planet, such as its colour or number, and strengthening yourself thereby. The stronger you are, then the more frequently you will be able to achieve the result you want—and that's all that luck is, isn't it?

A Final Word

By the time you reach here, you will have learnt a great deal more about yourself. At least, I hope you have.

You will probably have noticed that I appear to have contradicted myself in some parts of the book, and repeated myself in others, and there are reasons for this. It is quite likely that I have said that your Sun position makes you one way, while your Ascendant makes you the opposite. There is nothing strange about this; nobody is consistent, the same the whole way through—everybody has contradictory sides to their character, and knowing some more about your Sun sign and your Ascendant will help you to label and define those contradictory elements. It won't do anything about dealing with them, though—that's your job, and always has been. The only person who can live your horoscope is you. Astrology won't make your problems disappear, and it never has been able to; it simply defines the problems more clearly, and enables you to look for answers.

Where I have repeated myself it is either to make the point for the benefit of the person who is only going to read that section of the book, or because you have a double helping of the energy of your sign, as in the instance of the Sun and Ascendant in the same sign.

I hope you found the relationships section useful; you may well find that the Sun-to-Ascendant comparison is just as useful in showing you how you fit in with your partner as the usual Sun-to-Sun practice.

Where do you go from here? If you want to learn more about astrology, and see how all of the planets fit into the picture of the sky as it was at your birth, then you must either consult an astrologer or learn how to do it for yourself. There is quite a lot of astrology around these days; evening classes are not too hard to find and there are groups of enthusiasts up and down the country. There are also plenty of books which will show you how to draw up and interpret your own horoscope. There is a reading list at the end of this book.

One thing about doing it yourself, which is an annoyance unless you are aware of it in advance: to calculate your horoscope properly you will need to know where the planets were in the sky when you were born, and you usually have to buy this data separately in a book called an ephemeris. The reason that astrology books don't have this data in them is that to include enough for everybody who is likely to buy the book would make the book as big as a phone directory, and look like a giant book of log tables, which is a bit off-putting. You can buy ephemerides (the plural) for any single year, such as the one of your birth. You can also buy omnibus versions for the whole century.

So, you will need two books, not one: an ephemeris, and a book to help you draw up and interpret your horoscope. It's much less annoying when you *know* you're going to need two books.

After that, there are lots of books on the more advanced techniques in the Astrology Handbook series, also from the Aquarian Press. Good though the books are, there is no substitute for being taught by an astrologer, and no substitute at all for practice. What we are trying to do here is provide a vocabulary of symbols taken from the sky so that you and your imagination can make sense of the world you live in; the essential element is your imagination, and you provide that.

Astrology works perfectly well at Sun sign level, and it works perfectly well at deeper levels as well; you can do it with what you want. I hope that, whatever you do with it, it is both instructive and satisfying to you—and fun, too.

SUNS AND LOVERS

The Astrology of Sexual Relationships

Penny Thornton. It doesn't seem to matter how experienced –
or inexperienced – you are, when it comes to love and romance
there just *isn't* a fool proof formula. . . but this book does its best
to provide one! THE definitive astrological guide to sexual
relationships, this book is based upon the accumulated wisdom,
and observations of centuries of dedicated astrologers. Reveals:

- In-depth analysis of astrological types
- Male and female profiles for each star sign
- Zodiacal attitudes to intimate relationships
- Most compatible – and incompatible – partners

Each general star sign analysis is concluded with amazingly
frank reflections, often based upon personal interviews, with
many famous personalities including: Bob Champion; Suzi
Quatro; Colin Wilson; Jeremy Irons; HRH The Princess Anne;
HRH The Duke of York; Martin Shaw; Barbara Cartland; Twiggy
and many more. Written in an easy-to-read style, and packed
with illuminating and fascinating tit-bits, this book is compulsive
reading for anyone likely to have *any sort* of encounter with the
opposite sex!